What they say about Wendy
New Business in 90 Days and Ke

"There has never been a book like it. It is incredibly

—Lorraine Be

Developme

"Wendy Evans' concept and approach to our project was right on target. She helped us design a direct marketing lead generation campaign to build awareness of our products. Wendy did an outstanding job."

—Donna Conforti, Product Director,
Johnson and Johnson HMI, New Jersey.

"Wendy Evans' outstanding achievement was on Procter and Gamble's Pampers product. She conceived and directed a complex name-gathering program that was dramatically successful in its own right and in terms of product sales."

—Robert Fletcher, Managing Director,
Saatchi & Saatchi, Hong Kong.

"Wendy Evans took full responsibility for our marketing activities and promotional material. She developed a target list of 8000 names whom we contacted every 90 days with telemarketing follow-up for appointment setting. In the execution of this she excelled. We credit Wendy with our success."

—Marshall Jeanes, Vice Chairman,
IMCOR, New York

"*How to Get New Business in 90 Days and Keep It Forever* is an eminently sensible, well-written book with compelling quotes and good one-liners. As you turn the pages you steadily come across sound advice which you once heard, meant to remember, did not. Heaven knows what would happen if too many people jumped on the Wendy Evans band wagon. Perhaps it should be sold with a self-destruct button."

—Sir Clement Freud, London.

"I congratulate Wendy Evans on an exceptional book. Every page is convincing. All the points made are easily taken on board and clearly expressed. The book develops the art of persistence into fine-tuned skills. Chapter by chapter, fears are systematically changed into formulas for success."

—Dr Henry Nowik, Distinguished Research
Professor, International Business Diplomacy,
Georgetown University, Washington, D.C.

"Two of Wendy Evans' most substantial achievements were the development of the Thomas Cook World Travel Club and the customer information retrieval system. Her commercial acuity and wide experience have been crucial in underpinning their success."

—Kevin Gavaghan, Thomas Cook Travel, Australia.

"What a great piece of writing! For the first time I found a book that takes the mystique out of marketing. This book will be of immense value to both the experienced marketing specialist and the uninitiated.

"It makes easy reading and presents a plethora of stimulating and illuminating information. Unlike most other texts on the subject, I had difficulty in putting the book down."
—Ron Mantel, Business Manager, School of Tourism and Hospitality, Canberra Institute of Technology.

"*How to Get New Business in 90 Days and Keep It Forever* is an incisive, commonsense book for the moment; a book that should be read, re-read and used again and again. I can recommend this programme to any organisation."
—Ted Wright, Director and General Manager, Regent Hotel, Sydney.

"I found myself getting excited as I read, thinking, 'Yes, yes, this is what we need for the plans we have for Kmart'."
—Bob Dalziel, Managing Director, Kmart, Australia.

"Your course has equipped me with some new skills that are formidable. It is like discovering the pot of gold at the end of the rainbow."
—André du Chenne, Managing Director, Kagiso Khulani Supervision Food Services, South Africa.

"At last some grass-roots skills that can be implemented immediately."
—Trevor Phillips, Communication Development, Amalgamated Banks of South Africa.

"It's like finding a diamond in the desert."
—Bristol Myers Squibb sales staff, South Africa.

How to Get New Business in 90 Days and Keep It Forever

Wendy Evans

ZEBRA

First published in South Africa by Zebra Press
an imprint of Struik Publishers
(A division of New Holland Publishing (South Africa) (Pty) Ltd)
PO Box 1144, Cape Town, 8000
New Holland Publishing is a member of the Johnnic Publishing Group

First published in 1993 by Millennium Books
an imprint of E.J. Dwyer (Australia) Pty Ltd
Revised and expanded edition 1997
Reprinted in 1999 and 2001 by New Holland Publishers (Australia) Pty Ltd

ISBN 1 86872 369 0

10 9 8 7 6 5 4 3 2
Cover design by Mango Design Group
Text design by Midland Typesetters, Maryborough, Australia
Typeset in Palatino 11/13pt by Midland Typesetters
Printed in Australia by Griffin Press, Adelaide

www.zebrapress.co.za

Contents

Thank You

> *"A life spent making mistakes is not only more honourable but more useful than a life spent doing nothing."*
> George Bernard Shaw (1856–1950)

My thanks are unbounded—firstly to David Miln of Saatchi & Saatchi, London, because you were always there to share, discuss, argue and feed my zeal.

To Stuart and Sue Sanders, Sanders Consulting, Richmond, Virginia, USA, for training me in their new-business modules. Their work appears here in the sections on the four main personality styles. Nowhere else have I met such dedication to the business of doing new business well. I am proud to have known you and worked with you.

To Paul Dinte and staff of Morgan & Banks in Washington, for asking me to consult with them on this business development model. It was Paul who uttered that immortal line, "Why don't you write the book?" I realised then that "it" had come together . . . that the winning mix was at hand and that writing the book would now be fun (which it was).

To Wendy Braund, who typed and retyped the book and kept me going when I faded out; fed me, watered me and contributed to every section—particularly her own on "How to keep yourself organised".

To Nancy Rodriguez of IMCOR in New York, who backstopped me every step of the way and who also put the book into the office computer so I could work any time new ideas came to mind—and so often they did, late at night.

To Jo Kaufmann, my New York editor, for editing the book as though it were her own and making me realise that speaking and writing are different skills. Jo put down her own book to recreate mine, a much-valued and appreciated kindness.

To Robert Byrne, on whose excellent collection of quotations I drew: *1,911 Best Things Anybody Ever Said*, Fawcett Columbine, New York, 1988.

To W Mitchell, from whose splendid person and excellent book, *The Man Who Would Not Be Defeated*, I drew inspiration and quotations. Knowing you makes defeat impossible.

To all who commented on and reviewed the book, including: Rodney Adler, FAI; Michael Ball, The Ball Partnership; Helen Barr, Heirloom Designs; Ian Burns, Morgan and Banks; Philip Brass, Pacific Dunlop; Reg Bryson, The Campaign Palace; Marilyn Cummins, Bain & Co.; David Clark, S.A. Brewing Holdings; Donna Conforti, Johnson & Johnson HMI; Lynne De Weaver, De Weaver Integrated Advertising; John Fawcett, George Patterson Pty Ltd.

Also Sir Clement Freud; Wendy Greiner, S.A. Brewing Holdings; Helen Hill, Dunhill Management Services; Russ Ingersoll, TASA; Vin Jenkins, Clemenger Direct; Guy Kawasaki, author of *Selling the Dream;* Andrew Linklater, K & D Bond International; Bill Lodge, Wunderman Cato Johnson.

Plus Dr Henry Nowik, Mars, Inc., and Georgetown University; John Reid, Thomas Cook; David Say, James Hardie Industries; Willem Sprokkreeff, Hilton Hotels; Dr Leonie Still, University of Western Sydney, and Dr Michael Hewitt-Gleeson, Melbourne.

You made it what it is today.

And thank you to those who bought this book. It is dedicated to everyone who wants to grow their business. It comes with many years of travelling, many years of good times learning and achieving with some very talented people.

Dedication

To all the companies I have worked with, their managers and their staff, in America, England, Hong Kong, Australia, New Zealand and South Africa.

Without your trust and support there would never have been anything to write home about.

About Wendy Evans

> *"If I had my life to live again, I would make the same mistakes, only sooner."* Tallulah Bankhead (1902–1968)

Wendy Evans is an international marketer, consultant, trainer, professional speaker and author. She has spent the last fifteen years within major corporations, refining, analysing and improving the twelve steps of her book in Hong Kong, London, New York, Washington, Australia, New Zealand and South Africa.

From her experiences with local and international clients such as Royal Life Insurance UK, the Inter-Continental and Peninsula Hotel Groups, Procter and Gamble, British Airways, Johnson & Johnson, Saatchi & Saatchi, Thomas Cook, 3M and Vodacom, she wrote *How to Get New Business in 90 Days and Keep It Forever*, and developed the training and speaking programs that support it. The first edition climbed to second place on the Australian best-seller list.

Wendy's single-minded mission during these continuing years of travel has been to identify and refine relevant strategies and tactics for increasing new business, by regularly and relentlessly targeting potential clients and maintaining a continuous and creative follow-up program leading to closure.

The book and her workshops on the twelve steps to business success express her findings, and are guaranteed to help you create regular new-business opportunities throughout the lifetime of your company.

Introduction

How this book came to be written

> *"There is only one thing about which I am certain and that is that there is very little about which one can be certain."*
> W. Somerset Maugham (1874–1965)

I was accidentally successful, I decided. Yes, within a year of my joining the Inter-Continental Hotel Group in Melbourne the sales of room nights into their hotels around the world had grown ten-fold. Within eighteen months of my representing The Peninsula Group properties in Australia, their Hong Kong hotels were thirty per cent full of Australians, up from two per cent previously.

Yes, Thomas Cook had around twenty per cent of Australia's travel business with around three per cent of the travel offices. Yes, Newman's winter coach tour sales to New Zealand via the Thomas Cook travel offices increased from thirty to three hundred and fifty bookings over three years. Cruise bookings for all shipping lines had gone through the roof after the joint Thomas Cook/Sitmar disco at Blacktown . . . but why had these and many other activities that I had created and managed been so successful?

Some of the reasons were obvious. We combined sales promotion offers with direct marketing to bring forward the purchase decision. We kept an up-to-date database of transactions and client preferences. We shared that database with suppliers so that we could reach their market with a rifle shot into target-market homes, instead of the scatter gun approach of me-too advertising. We advised and rewarded the selling and support staff on a regular basis. We constantly reported back results in order to maintain the momentum. All this helped.

And it was incredibly hard work . . . that was the difficult part. I never quite knew why I was successful; I always wondered in the back of my mind if this time the promotion would not be the outrageous success I myself had come to expect. Then of course, clients expected it too. If the results didn't double year after year, there was this shocked surprise.

Somewhere out there, someone knew something that I needed to know. And in the time-honoured tradition I felt it would be overseas. What if I went away with the intent to spend around two years in each of several countries, looking, listening and learning, until I tracked down the key elements to commercial success?

Lao Tzu says, "The longest journey starts with a single step." My friend Henry Nowik of Georgetown University adds, "In the right direction". My right direction was to leave my clients and Sydney behind and join Saatchi & Saatchi Advertising in Hong Kong. There I took on the immense pleasure (and more hard work) of repositioning Procter & Gamble's Pampers product. During that time I analysed just what it was that went into doubling and tripling sales: what the steps were and how best to describe them.

After Hong Kong I moved on to London with Saatchi & Saatchi and joined their executive recruitment company, MSL, for a major new-business program. Then to New York to reposition IMCOR, a contract-leasing company specialising in placing very senior executives in temporary positions. For nearly six years I practised and refined the arts of business success—by really trying. Then I went back to Sydney to write this book.

> *"We don't know a millionth of one percent about anything."* Thomas Alva Edison (1847–1931)

In Hong Kong with Saatchi & Saatchi I learned "the single-minded proposition". What quite simply does the product or service do for the purchaser? No creative work could begin until we had all agreed on this; the client, the account-handling team and the creative people. Then everything we created was judged against the single-minded proposition agreed upon.

Recently I was giving a training session on what I now call

"the simple-minded proposition". (I call it this because it takes away the tension of being single-minded [overtones of authority there] and introduces an element of "anyone can do this".) I held a wonderful arrangement of red roses in my arms as I rang an imaginary doorbell. An imaginary woman answered, saw the roses in my arms and her big smile was all-embracing.

Having finished my role-playing, I asked the group in the room, "What was the benefit to you, the purchaser of these roses?" "Sex," said one of the men. "Romance," said one of the women. Next I rang the imaginary doorbell with a potted azalea in my arms. The woman's smile was less than beaming this time. I asked the group again, "What was the benefit to you, the purchaser of the azalea?"

After some thought, they suggested it might be an expression of friendship. The point here is that once you know the benefit or results desired, you match your strategy accordingly.

That's what I learnt from the single-minded proposition. It is not what you—in this case, the florist—think the product is; it is how the buyer, the person who parts with hard-earned money, really benefits from it.

In a recent workshop with a major advertising agency, we discussed starting a business selling red roses 24 hours a day, 365 days a year. The workshop group was to decide—by identifying the motives for sending red roses—what the business would be called, and what the tag line would be.

The group decided that the company name would be (of course) "Bad Boys" and the tag line would be "We get you into—and out of—trouble 24 hours a day."

A Minolta poster states its single-minded proposition very clearly. It says: "Minolta—we understand the office." Which is what we want from a company that supplies fax machines, photocopiers and laser printers. Ask yourself, what do you understand—from the client's point of view?

Staying in touch within ninety days was a natural for the disposable diaper that was my major responsibility in Hong Kong. Within three months babies outgrow their current disposable diaper size.

If the mothers don't know this, they blame the product when the baby "leaks" out of it. With nearly one hundred thousand mothers in the database, we were busy with communications and sales promotion offers to upgrade to the next size, to ensure that no such mishaps occurred.

Research in Germany showed that around fifty per cent of mothers stopped using disposable diapers after the first six months for a variety of reasons, one of them being the (apparent) failure of the product. With our ninety-day program of communication and offers, it was one less reason in Hong Kong.

It also reconfirmed my belief in what I later called "the Commonality Survey": you get more business from people who resemble those who are currently your best clients. Obviously mothers with babies are the only likely market for this size of disposable diaper. Yet research shows that many Hong Kong babies are still in diapers up to three years of age, the reason being that the Filipina maids do not speak Cantonese so do not encourage the babies to change their ways. They simply do what they can until such time as the baby is old enough to understand the parents' wishes.

This fact known, an even bigger size of diaper has been manufactured and promoted and the parents have stayed loyal to Pampers for three years and more.

For a long time I had been involved in business plans and noticed that they required a huge amount of work, then were put in a cupboard somewhere and left to rot while all involved rushed around putting out fires and hoping for the best.

Business/marketing plans seemed to work when they were done on a *product basis,* while taking into account the overall needs of the organisation. Such was the disposable diaper business plan for making it the top-selling product of its kind in Hong Kong.

From that experience I formulated the policy that every product I undertake to promote, as a consultant, has to have its own business/marketing plan, very like the outline provided further on in this book. Done in as few words as possible, it stays on the desk and is a working model for where we are going and how we are doing. Because it focuses down into one product, one market (approximately), it is likely that we can convince the client of the benefits to be gained by the time and the cost involved.

Time and cost are not as much a problem with the big multinational companies as they are with young, entrepreneurial start-up companies where the owners have a good idea they believe the world will want now. The fact is, however, that the outside world can—and often does—take three to five years to notice that bright new product or service, assuming that there are enough funds to promote and advertise for that period.

No client ever wants to hear that, I learned, which is even more reason to have the business/marketing plan agreed to before work is commenced.

> *"The purpose of life is a life of purpose."* Robert Byrne

In London I heard that Saatchi's had a magic system for new business. They have been using it for over twenty years, and it made them one of the biggest advertising agencies in the world. So I met David Miln, David who invented the "canal boat process", where a wide band of prospects are contacted within ninety days.

This was when I found confirmation for the ninety days process that I had been practising in Hong Kong and had learned myself during my years with the Inter-Continental Hotel Group in Melbourne.

When David said that over many years they had found that less than three months without contacting was fine, but after more than three months the prospects forget about you, I could see so clearly that graph of room night sales in Melbourne.

I remember how the huge increases I achieved in room night sales to Inter-Continental Hotels worldwide, the result of my year of hard work calling on the travel industry, collapsed on the fourth month when I had been kept in the office researching and writing training programs.

For three months all the travel consultants had remained loyal, with bookings holding on at that absolutely highest point, waiting for me to come back on sales calls. The fourth month, when I did not show up, they gave up and responded to the Hilton Group instead.

Bookings out of Melbourne into the Inter-Continental hotels worldwide crashed faster in that fourth month than they had grown in twelve. And here was confirmation from David Miln at Saatchi & Saatchi. We agreed that within three months—or less—you are building relationships but after three months your clients and prospects are again very receptive to your competitors.

Furthermore, as I found with the Inter-Continental experience, if they have really grown to trust and like you and then you apparently walk out on them, they give everything and more to the next caller as a reaction against you for betraying that trust.

Moral of the story is: if you start on new-business prospecting you must stay within the three-month cycle, or you are wasting your money. Less than three months is fine; more than three months you might as well tear the money up and throw it to the winds. Stay with the new-business activities or you will lose more than you gain. You can't get off once you get on.

> *"Talk is cheap because supply exceeds demand."* Unknown

Two years in Hong Kong and two years in London taught me a lot, including some basic but important ways for improving my telephone skills. A great deal of the business of doing new business involves the telephone. A number of the telephone relationships we have with other people are unpleasant, to say the least.

Again David Miln of Saatchi's taught us good and simple things: be sure you know why are you making the phone call; never sell on the **first** phone call . . . only open up the opportunity of a meeting; stand up while phoning—you will sound powerful and in control.

Smile when you speak—the way you sound is directly related to the way your mouth is. Down is miserable, up is happy. Keep good notes. Dress well to feel good on the phone. Be polite. Always be the last to hang up.

From all over the world and with a great helping hand from British Telecom I collected the best of telephone tips. These are included in the section on "Success in your calling cycles".

> *"I'm in a phone booth at the corner of Walk and Don't Walk."* Unknown

In London in August, 1990, I met with the Managing Director of a recently created company in New York, who was referred to me by Saatchi's. He (John Thompson) was looking to expand into

Europe but also had a need for a sophisticated marketing program for his company in New York.

And so, on cue, I was on the next leg of my journey: to New York, where my first activity was to redesign and reposition their corporate look and feel. I became very interested in the meaning of colours relative to imagery and thought back to the most colourful time of my life: Hong Kong.

> *"What a time! What a civilisation!"* Cicero (106–43 BC)

While living in Hong Kong I noticed an intensity of interest in colour and design of clothing and in the design of hotels, shops, restaurants. Life is an endless quest for image. It is blatant. Everyone is judged by personal presentation. Position is clarified by property and accessories as proven, for instance, by the way traffic in Hong Kong manages itself.

There, whatever status of car you drive, drivers of that same status will let you in, as roads merge and disappear in the endless rebuilding that goes on. If you drive a little car, all other little cars will let you in. If you drive a middle-of-the-road Mazda or Toyota, all other middle-of-the-road cars will let you in.

If you drive a Rolls, Jaguar, Mercedes, BMW or Ferrari, all those, too, will let you in. When coming to a merge point you simply look back, wait until "your" kind of car arrives and there you are, neatly merged. But don't try it until you are safely in your class, because it won't happen.

I asked myself, if this unwritten law works so well for traffic, then it must work for promotional material too. Sure, we all know junk mail when we see it and throw it out in disgust, but what about all those dull and boring images that financial institutions (other than some building societies) present to us? All those greys and blacks and smudgy greens?

Perhaps, I thought, only grey and black and smudgy green people are going to let those companies into their lives. Bright and shiny people, powerful people, will want their chosen corporations to look more like them.

Kandinsky, I said to myself! Kandinsky did wonderful things with colour and I wanted to know what he knew. As I had that thought, that moment of truth, in New York, I found myself beside a second-hand bookstore. I wheeled in and there found his book on his thoughts regarding the effect that colour has on people.

When you read the section on colour in "Look like the company you want to be", you will see my retranslation and reworkings of that dusty little book in New York. Now you too can look like the company you want to be, simply by choosing the right colour—the colour that represents the business you are in, in the eyes of your kind of consumer.

Another day I joined a tour at the Metropolitan Museum in New York. We were looking at a painting where the main figure, in a beam of sunlight, was wearing a bright, pure red coat. The other figures were in shadowy black.

The guide was saying, "You see the power of this red coat? The eye always goes to the point of greatest contrast. The artist has drawn you to the picture with that one red figure. You have no choice but to see the red coat first, then continue into the picture to see the supporting characters."

I knew about the single-minded proposition and the corporate statement that flows from that. Now I knew how to make people read it. I had only to make the words the point of greatest contrast, the largest piece of copy on the first-seen part of any promotional piece I was preparing, and regardless of your intent, you would be drawn to read that message first.

Any subsidiary message I would make smaller and therefore less intense in contrast so that your eye would go there next.

I have used this technique ever since—and ever since it has worked. It came to me slowly but surely from my driving experience in Hong Kong. "When the student is ready, the teacher comes."

At the New York firm, IMCOR, I used all the techniques I had acquired to research the best of their existing client base in order to find the right kind of prospects, plus my colour, design, layout, copywriting and telephone techniques.

And I learned about the left- and right-hand side of the brain and how to position words and graphics for greatest effect. You'll find it all in that "Look like the company you want to be" section and it has all worked for me and my clients.

The emphasis on maintaining a competitive edge, making relevant special offers and being flexible in contract negotiations came about from my time at the Sales Machine. This was a company that specialised in sales promotion, where purchase decisions were encouraged by the use of special offers.

Combined with the rifle-shot activities of direct marketing, with the processes and results captured in a database, the results of sales promotion can be spectacular. We increased the sales of Pampers in Hong Kong by US$29 million in just over a year, for instance.

Yes, we advertised as well and that was a necessary part of being seen in all media. However, the main thrust was database marketing with special offers. Time-consuming and highly detailed it may be, but it is very measurable and effective.

Over a lifetime of work and family matters, I have seen too many contracts that treated the buyer like the enemy. So I have included a section in this book on improving contracts and therefore the ongoing business relationship, ever after.

Saatchi & Saatchi are the masters of PR—of endless, single-minded PR about their creativity and the success of that creativity for their clients.

They walked their talk in London, bringing out one great advertising campaign after another.

They were audacious for clients and for themselves in their mergers and acquisitions. They made news where other advertising agencies could not even find the words for similar successes. Saatchi's are the masters of "the squeaky wheel" process: the more noise you make, the more attention you get.

I am reminded of the story about the hen and the salmon. The hen lays a single egg and cackles so loudly that everyone within hearing rushes out and exclaims over her cleverness. The salmon, responding to the long-ago memories of the scents of her birthplace, swims hundreds of kilometres through oceans, up rushing rivers, over wild waterfalls into the quiet waters of her birth. She lays thousands of eggs and dies, unnoticed, in the shallows.

Saatchi's is the hen. A single egg to them is worth a million laid by other more silent companies. You choose. You don't have to do anything brilliant, just be single-minded about your PR processes. Use the section in this book called "The regular follow-up". Make yourself stand head and shoulders above your competition.

"How to keep yourself organised" is a section contributed by my very organised friend, Wendy Braund. Having recently taken two years out for an MBA, she puts into practice all the skills she offers in this section. Of all the tips on offer, I most enjoy the one that suggests using different coloured files and paper for the different areas of your responsibilities. It brightens up the desk and makes for instant recognition.

Other colourful examples: I was asked to design a form for telephone sales staff, taking travel bookings in England. We analysed the actions into three main sections and printed a few as a test run in black and white. It was so boring to look at that we printed the three sections on three different shades of paper as another test. Now it glowed on the desk and was inviting to the staff, instead of being dull and dreary.

At the Auckland and Tahiti Inter-Continental Hotels we had a problem with the white room rate sheets for next year looking exactly like the white room rate sheets for the current year. Wholesalers, being confused, were working on the cheaper rates and trouble ensued. So we threw out all of the next year's rate sheets and redid them on coloured paper. End of problem.

> *"I took a course in speed reading and was able to read* War and Peace *in twenty minutes. It's about Russia."*
>
> Woody Allen

Time management is included in the section on organisation and I finally came to terms with what that subject was about when I read Stephen Covey's "7 Habits of Highly Effective People".

In that book he says that only when you have a clear set of objectives can you manage your time well, because the objectives themselves define the use of your time. Any other interruption, distraction or better offer for the use of your time is then measured against what will happen to your objectives if you deviate.

Being effective rather than being efficient is important. Many people do their chosen portion of work efficiently but do not manage effectively. I have met people who would be just as likely to prioritise their funeral before they got round to being born.

Persistence pays, according to David Miln and me and all the people whom I have ever known to be successful. David says that if you make three times more new-business telephone calls than your competitors, you are four times more successful.

How many people do you know who always make three

new-business phone calls a day? It is not hard to be four times more successful ... you just have to pick up the phone more often!

> *"Money is good for bribing yourself through the inconveniences of life."* Gottfried Reinhardt

"Nothing changes" is a common expression but when I was enlightened by Stuart Sanders of Sanders Consulting in Richmond, Virginia, about the four main personality types, everything changed.

Understanding the personalities of the people you deal with on a daily basis eases the pain. How come these weird, rude people belong to the human race when you and I are so polite, pleasant and well-mannered?—well, most of the time.

I used to dread phoning the accountant at a particular client company. After I got "enlightened" I rang him with delight, just to reassure myself that his abrupt, curt, flat manner was still there and he was still conforming to his personality type. I got quite fond of him after a while, when I stopped reacting against him. But as far as he was concerned, he was just being his usual busy self.

The material on the four main personality types in "Keep your clients forever" is there for you to learn to enjoy/understand all those people you never enjoyed/understood before. Also another new skill—that of Neurolinguistics. A profound shift for me again, when I found that people are different in personalities and different in the way they give out and take in information.

Perhaps we too can reach Nirvana with our newly found enlightenment.

> *"It is better to know some of the questions than all of the answers."* James Thurber (1894–1961)

So now, in more detail, let's look at the twelve steps that I believe are the key to business success. Many of them I learned from Saatchi's; all of them I learned because I was looking for answers.

These answers came along with the realisation that it is enough to want something for it to arrive. But to get what you want takes time, energy and money (as does almost everything worth having).

You can succeed in business, but you really have to try. Good luck and good hunting. See, hear and feel success.

The twelve steps for success

> *"If it weren't for the last minute, nothing would get done."* Unknown

These twelve steps, in part, made Saatchi & Saatchi the number one advertising agency in the world; increased Procter & Gamble's market share of Pampers in Hong Kong by US$19 million in fourteen months; helped British Airways merge the British Caledonian clients into the BA world in Hong Kong and lead Asia in their promotional activities and turned MSL International into a major marketing force in executive recruitment in England.

With these twelve steps, IMCOR in New York became market leader in contract management in America; Johnson & Johnson was positioned for a major telemarketing campaign for their Live for Life product in America; Morgan and Banks created a new contact management and marketing process in Washington and Thomas Cook achieved up to twenty per cent market share with around three per cent of the travel offices in Australia.

Now these techniques are yours to grab and run with; to use to seek out, make contact with, develop and retain new clients and customers for your business.

In good times or bad, all businesses need more clients. In good times new clients should replace the ones lost through attrition. In bad times new clients can help your business survive. Yet, during good years we are too short of time to conduct new-business activities. In bad years we are too worried and too financially strapped to think about more expenditure.

The fact is, however, that the Saatchi & Saatchi new-business system can be readily and cost-effectively put into operation in good times or bad. Once in place, it won't matter whether you are too busy or too worried; the new-business process will simply march on, budgeted in as part of your regular operations, keeping you in profit for your lifetime.

The twelve steps apply to companies of all sizes, wherever they do business. This book is based on the premise that relationship-building, trust and fair dealing are paramount to the success of a company's health and wealth. The twelve steps will provide practical knowledge that can be applied to begin or maintain existing business and to develop valuable new business, whether you are starting up or wanting to expand.

> *"Cogito ergo spud—I think therefore I yam."* Graffito

Step one: You must have a set of goals with actions and costs for the future, a strategic plan by which to guide your business and promotional plans for your individual product or service. This can easily be achieved by this simple technique. You can see the future by standing there and looking backwards to today.

Start with that end in mind and write your marketing and business plans accordingly. Where do you want to be in a few years' time? What actions do you need to take to make it happen?

A friend of mine used to say, "Beware of what you want, for you shall surely get it." Just sitting down and thinking your way through the actions for success will generate that success. Then write these actions, timing and costs down, to "carve them in stone" and commit yourself to action.

Step two: Build a broad base of prospects. Sales people can be choking the life out of too few prospects. Don't get caught up in pursuing twenty prospects when you can be gently nudging two hundred or more. You will likely have had the experience yourself of being hotly pursued and then dumped if you did not obey "their" demands for you to buy their product, now.

Don't let that sense of being held by the throat happen to your prospects. People don't mean "no", they mean "not now". What is important is that you are still there when it is the right time for them to buy.

Step three: Define your prospect base. Good new prospects can look very like your current excellent clients. The Commonality Survey section will help you find your future best prospects, by looking at the common elements of your current best clients.

Of likely key importance is their proximity to your place of business, your understanding of their product or service and whether or not they pay their bills. After that your greatest success will come from the people whom you understand, respect and enjoy being with.

I stress being near to you because it is the same in business as with your friends—you see more of the ones nearby than those across the river, over the railway line, out of town.When people feel near to you, they are more likely to phone you, drop by, give you business. Also the cost of doing business is less on both sides.

An example: in Sydney an advertising agency told me of a great relationship they had lost. After many happy years the client had moved from directly opposite to five kilometres away. Within the year that client had moved to another agency closer by.

If you are starting out in business, it is day one and you have no clients to research for their common characteristics, then research your nearest competitor's clients and create a profile from them. Pretend you are your competitor and their business is yours. When you have seen what is the norm, you can then step outside it with innovative ideas for developing your product to attract new types of clients and customers.

> *"We can't all be heroes because somebody has to sit on the curb and clap as they go by."* Will Rogers, 1879–1935

Step four: Three is the proven number; make contact with your prospects within three months. We seem to know innately that "three" is the way to go. Don't seasons have three months? Don't we say, "Third time lucky"; "Try, try, try again"? New-business activities must be ongoing over the life of your company, not a stop-start-stop activity. Proven by Saatchi & Saatchi over a twenty-year test period and during my time with Inter-Continental Hotels, ninety days—or less—is the cycle for building relationships.

Remember what it is like when you get a call from someone you met, say, two years ago and haven't heard from since? They invite you to lunch and you know three things absolutely: they are in trouble and want your help and you will end up paying for lunch. This is not the reaction you want people to have to you. Building relationships slowly with contact over a period of time creates trust and takes away the sense of "This is going to hurt".

Step five: You must know what it is, quite simply, that your company provides, from the client's point of view. With the "single-minded proposition" finalised, you can then create an umbrella statement for all your future corporate communications.

Without it, you have no guidelines with which to brief your advertising, PR, sales promotion and direct marketing staff or agencies. Again, if you are just beginning to think about starting your own business, do this exercise for competitors' businesses until you get it right for yours.

Start by asking what it is that your favourite store, restaurant, hotel or car, provides for you. This has nothing to do with the obvious statements like "provides clothing/food/a bed to sleep in/a mode of getting around the place". It has everything to do with courteous service, a great atmosphere, value for money, and the feel of the power and the wind in your hair. A sense of wanting more.

When you know why customers return to you, what it is you give them that benefits them and makes them want more, then you have your single-minded proposition.

> *"I base my fashion on what doesn't itch."* Gilda Radner

Step six: Look like the company you want to be. Make your entity enticing to staff, prospects and clients. Use design and colour to make your company look solid and stable or new and exciting. The image your company conveys by its decor and written materials is received in a split second.

I was invited into a boardroom recently. It was done out in dull green and black with those very uncomfortable black leather chairs that slope back, causing you to fold into an agonised V shape. We all preferred to stand and we joked that probably nobody had sat in one of those chairs more than once, ever.

The company is shortly moving to new premises and we discussed the new decor. Their brief to the interior design consultant was to decorate the new offices—and particularly the new boardroom—to reflect their transition from a small company to a successful, bigger company, settling into prosperity but still reflecting their hallmark of creativity.

Our next question was: what will happen to clients and prospective clients in that brief? It will, after all, be human beings who enter the room, not the company's transition.

Then we thought through the decor in terms of standing in the boardroom and looking out across their large terrace and into the sky and harbour beyond. How about a sense of soaring with the eagles, of light and weightlessness, where all your worries are left behind on earth? Since that meeting I have seen the agreed plans and they do reflect all this and more, as well as the transition of the company. So everything is possible with the right architect and designer.

Step seven: Your "sound" is important, too. If you heard yourself or your staff broadcast live on radio in your daily dealings with clients, suppliers and prospects, would you be pleased and proud?

Try this simple activity: leave your office and go to the office of an understanding business acquaintance with a speaker phone. Listen while your friend rings your office and asks for you/wants to leave a message/wants the fax number/asks even for your home number. See if your staff are pleasant and courteous or offhanded and rushed. Then again, have that same friend pose as a buyer of your product or service and see what sort of response the staff feels competent to give.

In New York I used to ring a company where one of the telephonists was from hell. I commented to a visitor from their London head office that she was definitely the worst I had ever come across and he replied that they had had many complaints about her over the years! Nothing had been done, of course, but they were at least aware of the problem!

> *"We are what we pretend to be."* Kurt Vonnegut, Jr

Step eight: Defend your right to be absolutely consistent in your corporate messages—even to the point of boring yourself (but not others). Keep your regular follow-up messages the same, endlessly. Do not confuse your listener/viewer with new sounds, new colours, new messages.

Why be boring? Why not? Coca-Cola is probably boring to the people who work there and to the advertisers at times, but to us, the consumers, it is endlessly the same in its logo and sexy fun image. We know and love Coca-Cola.

We know and love McDonald's, Kentucky Fried Chicken and Pizza Hut, too, and I personally love the Regent Hotels with a passion—not because they advertise endlessly, but because they behave in the same stupendously excellent way wherever I am lucky enough to experience them. I don't know if they ever get bored with being perfect; I certainly love it. If you are onto a good thing, stick with it. If you have your doubts (where is that telephonist from hell?), then do something about it!

Step nine: Maintain a competitive edge by making effective and continuous special offers to move product and bring forward the purchase decision in your favour. Be flexible, be understanding of the other person's needs and wants, ahead of your own. Then you win too.

Think back to your experiences in purchasing and contracting for major items, like a house, a car, furniture, additions to your home. Recall the experience of signing these purchase orders or business contracts for employment, premises, equipment, whatever.

You loved every one of these purchases and/or contract negotiations, didn't you? No? Some of them? Maybe one? Not even one? Think what it would have been like if all the transactions had been friendly and courteous. You were spending a lot of money, almost putting your life on the line and wouldn't it have been great if they had acknowledged that by offering some relevant gift to mark the occasion?

Imagine if they had sat down with you to look at the contract together and invited you to comment on anything that caused you concern! Then suppose they had expressed their willingness to cooperate—and meant it!

Now look at your own selling and contract processes. See if from now on you can make the experience a great one on both sides.

> *"I think it would be a good idea."* Mahatma Ghandi (1869–1948), when asked what he thought of Western civilisation

Step ten: Be organised. All the other steps will be of no use if you're unable to manage your time. One of the best tips I have come across in time management is to divide the number of projects you have on your desk by the number of minutes in your working day. If you have fifty projects, you can give each eight minutes. You can make a lot of decisions and shift a lot of "monkeys" off your back in that time, as well as go to lunch.

If you are a solo operator or running a business with few staff, you can find you have too many things to do, all the time. Try to do whatever is relatively unimportant first so that they never become important. Make your new-business phone calls, send thank-you notes and follow-up faxes, organise that lunch date, handle that complaint, chase people who owe you money.

Similarly other "little" things like salary reviews, performance reviews, rostering time out for training and holidays and regular maintenance of equipment—all these take on a life of their own when ignored. Do a few of these "unimportant" things every day and they will never become a major issue ... they will just flow on as part of your processes each morning.

Manage your time to be effective. Understand the difference between "important" and "urgent". Beware of people who rush in and interrupt your work to push their "urgent" work onto you. It might be urgent for them, but perhaps it is important for you to keep on with your tasks. If you stop to help them, will you stop being effective for yourself?

Do a business plan for your company and manage your time to meet those objectives. Anything that takes you away from meeting those goals is potentially damaging to the health and success of your business. Say no, from a position of strength.

Also ask yourself if you are doing the job your superiors expect you to do. In London we researched that particular subject in one of our working parties and found that most staff felt their job was very different from the one their boss thought they should be doing.

Even if they had performance reviews, the goalposts were shifted each time until they did not know where they stood.

Clarify your position so all parties concerned are in agreement, and keep clarifying it. The world moves so fast today that your work can change as you sleep.

In London at MSL, Saatchi's executive recruitment company, we ran a workshop on this performance review issue and a suggested solution was to agree your goals with your subordinates, your peer group and your superior. Then at review time only these agreed goals could be critiqued. Feedback was that it worked very well.

> *"You get what you focus on."* Anthony Robbins

Step eleven: Persistence pays. Start now and never give up. Imagine if you had started these twelve steps two years ago, how many new clients you would have by now! Similarly, if you stand forward two years and look back to this day, you will get an idea of how much you can achieve in that time, with regular, relentless, unchanging communications and courteous, caring follow-up.

> *"You are no bigger than the things that annoy you."*
> Jerry Bundsen

Step twelve: Understand your staff, clients and prospects by understanding yourself in terms of your personality and your personal communications style. Some people are magic to deal with, others awkward. When you understand yourself you understand what is going on around you.

Now I set out to understand others, to adapt, to find the right words for their needs. In my personal relationships I expect people to behave exactly the way they are. I try not to push the buttons that will upset them, or to get upset myself because they are not like me. Life is unbelievably easier.

Sometimes I suddenly realise that I am having the happiest time, the best fun talking with a person I have just met. Then I realise that we have the same personality style and way of giving out and taking in information. Other times I find myself thinking

I am overdoing my highly visual language, so I look for more hard-edged words or emotive language to describe the subject in the other person's style. It is not enough to have a vision—I have to describe it in their terms.

Three things to remember about being persistent, regularly and relentlessly

One: When people say "no", they usually mean "not now", if you have carefully chosen them as prospects. If on the other hand, you have grabbed a whole lot of names at random, they may well mean no.

Two: When they say "no", they say it to the opportunity, not to you.

Three: If you do not want to make those phone calls and are finding all sorts of excuses, it is because you believe that the prospects on the other end are saying "no" to you, not to the opportunity.

You have got it the wrong way around. Just a small change in your way of thinking and you really will stop caring about rejection.

It is not you who is being rejected, only the product or service you are offering at the time. When you think about it, the whole world says "no" to somebody or other all the time.

How many times have you felt more for a person than they have for you? How many times have you wanted attention and been told "not now"? Life's like that. And then it changes.

People do say "yes". Love is returned, help and attention are given, nice things happen unexpectedly including winning huge pieces of new business because you were there, regularly and relentlessly, building the relationship, taking "no" as meaning, "not now". And coming back for more.

A reminder of the twelve steps

1. Create powerful business and marketing plans that are realistic, congruent, relevant and flexible.
2. Open up a whole new universe of prospects, people most likely to buy.
3. Choose them wisely through the Commonality Survey.

4. Make regular, relentless contact within ninety days; build the relationship gently.
5. Create that critically important "single-minded proposition", to give your customer base their reason to buy from you.
6. Look like the solid, stable or bright, jazzy company you want to be.
7. Sound like the company you have chosen to be.
8. Get in there, stay in there, with regular relentless, repetitious follow-up.
9. Make great special offers to bring forward the purchase decision in your favour.
10. Be organised and manage your time well, knowing your objectives.
11. Be persistent. If you make three times more phone calls than your competitors, you will be four times more successful.
12. Keep your clients forever by understanding yourself and them.

Remember—you get what you focus on.

Step 1: Part A

Plan to succeed—through your SWOT analysis

> *"The breakfast of champions is not cereal, it is the opposition."*
> Nick Seitz

To create long-term success, it is time to pause and think strategically. Here's how.

Stand in the future and look back to today

A simple and very effective technique for planning the future for either business or personal needs is to to project yourself ahead in your mind's eye and then look back to "where you are today".

Pause now, look up from this book and travel to where you want to be in a few years, or a decade down the road. Consider where you are at that future time you have chosen. What have you achieved, what actions did you take to get there, what kind of financing did you require?

If you have trouble standing forward and looking back to today, draw a line in a shape that expresses how you see your business developing over the coming years. The line could go straight across for your business staying the same, or up (if you are optimistic), or down (if you are pessimistic).

From the vantage point of that time in the future, look back to where you are today and see what you must do to accomplish your projections. Adjust your current time scales, expenditures, actions and financial program to overcome any obstacles you may encounter in getting from "here" to "there".

When your vision from that future time is consistent with the time, money and actions required to get there, you will be able to move forward with confidence. To see the future and plan for it competently is that simple and also that difficult. When you have done it, you can write your marketing and business (or personal) plans accordingly.

Overview of a business plan

> *"When you become a star, you don't change, everybody else does."*
> Kirk Douglas

Since many companies don't have an actively used business plan (mostly they seem to be lying at the bottom of a filing cabinet somewhere) and all businesses need one, I now offer an outline and discussion of what I consider a business plan should include.

It is designed to help you begin the thinking process. Three books are recommended in the reading list at the back under the heading "Business Plans".

First you need a SWOT analysis of your business as it stands today, SWOT meaning Strengths, Weaknesses, Opportunities and Threats. In the case studies section of this book, you will read about how various companies identified their needs and then really did something about it.

For instance, with Procter & Gamble and their Pampers product, their strength was that they already had thirteen per cent of the disposable diaper market. They were therefore not starting off as a new product trying to enter a crowded market.

Their weakness was that they were new in the Asian market, and competitive products had the other eighty-seven per cent. The opportunity was to send in a new team and spend money wisely and well (since their budgets were limited). The threat was the other major brand disposable diapers that were competitive in price and quality and had market dominance.

In taking action, the P & G people decided that being market leader with Pampers was the only acceptable position. This was achieved in principle within fourteen months. The demand was such that they would have had fifty-two per cent of the market.

However, the factory could not keep up with this demand. In addition, we found that the product was being diverted from Hong Kong and sold on the black market in Taiwan. Pampers therefore stood at forty-two per cent of the market as I left to live in England.

Saatchi & Saatchi/MSL, an executive recruitment company in London, saw their strength as being a well-established, highly reputable company. Their weakness was that they had become complacent and lost market share over the last decade.

The opportunity was to retake the high ground and be visible again as market leaders. The threat was in the form of younger, more actively competitive companies who had taken over MSL's position.

The full weight of the twelve steps, as described in this book, was thrown against the problem to the extent that a business associate from Unilever commented that he had never previously heard of MSL and now was having nightmares about the company.

IMCOR in New York identified their strength as having a new product (interim management/executive leasing) that the marketplace wanted. Their weakness was that they had been relying on networking as their sales process and now realised that they had to expand their reach.

"We were running out of friends," to quote Chairman John Thompson. The opportunity was to become market leader in America and the threat was the length of time and costs it takes to get a new product up and running profitably.

> *"I have never liked working. To me a job is an invasion of privacy."* Danny McGoorty (1901–1970)

Five years is usually the minimum time required for that to occur. Again the full weight of these twelve steps was put into play and within eighteen months IMCOR had achieved market dominance and profitability. Was it coincidence that this happened about five years after the company had started out in business?

Thomas Cook in Australia had identified their strength as being their highly reputable name in the travel industry, but their weakness was that they had lost their market dominance in cruise bookings.

Also their traditional market of older English-background

clients was dying out. The opportunity was to expand their reach into the younger market, aged 35 and below. The threat was that many other companies were already in touch with the youth market and doing it well.

Realising this, Thomas Cook set out to attract the young market in a way that was highly personal and experiential, such as holding a disco in conjunction with Sitmar cruises. Interestingly, this strategy brought in the parents too and Thomas Cook achieved new dominance in P & O cruises, and Royal Viking cruises as well as Sitmar.

> *"It is really hard to be roommates with people if your suitcases are much better than theirs."* J.D. Salinger

The above SWOT examples are illustrated more fully through the case studies (last section). Here is one more, on Johnson & Johnson.

Johnson & Johnson USA diversified into another division called Health Management Inc, which offered health facilities from testing units to full-blown gymnasiums fully managed and operated by J & J HMI. Their strength was the parent name, and their product was immediately perceived as trustworthy and value for money.

Their weakness was that their most profitable market consisted of large organisations who wanted the whole lot through to the installation and management of a complete gymnasium, with supervised health and fitness for the thousands of staff they employed. This market was collapsing in on itself with one in three large companies re-forming each year, as opposed to one in ten in the previous decade.

The opportunity was to re-form J & J HMI itself by reviewing their product offerings against the abilities of the remaining corporations to pay, particularly in view of the recessionary times in America. The threats to J & J HMI were:

(1) The competition from other companies also offering in-house health care;

(2) Other gym facilities in which corporations could buy memberships at less than the cost of in-house programs;

(3) The delay in perceivable benefits as early statistics indicated that it took three years for a corporation's bottom line to reflect the increased wellbeing of its staff (and therefore less time off and fewer industrial accidents). Fewer corporations could now afford to wait that length of time—so the task was to reform the J & J product to suit this changing market.

Now begin to think through your own SWOT analysis. What are the strengths, weaknesses, opportunities and threats of your business? I recommend that you do your thinking in this exact order, beginning with strengths and weaknesses. I have occasionally reversed or shifted the order around to find out what would happen.

If I concentrate on the threats first, for instance, I find myself overly concerned because I am not coming at them from that beginning position of strength. Similarly, I see the opportunities far better if I acknowledge my strengths and weaknesses first. Finally, the threats seem quite small when the other three are in place.

> *"The advantage of emotions is that they lead us astray."*
> Oscar Wilde (1854–1900)

For you to define your key strategic and tactical issues, here is a SWOT analysis that I have used for myself and for clients. It is simple, it works and it also gives you a readout of the culture of your organisation. Since culture is a reflection of what goes on internally, you cannot change or fix the cultural issues unless you change or fix the key strategic and tactical issues.

You will note that you answer "true" or "not true" to the statements. If you answer "true" it is an issue to be discussed and changed; if you answer "not true" then it is not a problem—it's a positive aspect of your organisation. It's that simple—so go for it!

And when you have decided what your key strategic and tactical issues are, reflect upon them as if they were icebergs. It is only by going around the iceberg and down into the depths that you can see its full magnitude. Hence the more time you spend analysing what is causing the problems, the quicker you fix the problems at the other end.

Example: A company started up by three entrepreneurs had grown quickly and the staff had no clear understanding of the purpose and direction of the organisation. This was their key strategic issue. Also they had too many customer complaints because deliveries arrived later than promised. This was their key tactical issue.

The culture of the organisation was that everything was a priority, at the expense of proper planning, so they were reactive rather than proactive.

> *"There is no sweeter sound than the crumbling of one's fellow man."* Groucho Marx (1890–1977)

Penetrating the iceberg, I realised that the three entrepreneurs had never really talked through their individual visions for the future; they were in such harmony that they didn't need to. But their staff needed to know. To find the words for the strategic purpose and direction, I asked each of the owners to separately write down their key actions for the coming three years.

Then I asked them to give a score out of ten as to the importance of each activity in the coming three years. The activities were then written up in order of ranking and the staff brought in.

In a matter of minutes they absorbed the work on the blackboard, said, "Fine", and moved on to the key tactical issue, which was of course, the customer complaints.

Going deep into the iceberg they realised that they had too many customer complaints because they had grown so fast that their systems and procedures were not adequate for the volume of work going through. On the spot they appointed a staff member (with previous experience) to fix their systems and procedures.

Are they now proactive rather than reactive? Do they have time to plan well, because they are no longer putting out the fires of customer complaints? I hope so!

An important point relative to working parties for fixing particular problems or opening up new opportunities, or whatever: never, never go beyond eight people, preferably fewer.

Why? Think of a dinner party you have been to when there were ten or more people at the table. It split somewhere in the centre and turned into a "them and us" situation. It is exactly the same at work. Up to eight people is a functioning entity, after eight you have two separate groups, neither one of which is in communication with the other.

Strange but true. I have a friend who was one of twelve children and he said that they hardly spoke to each other, they were so divided—all of them.

> *"First secure an independent income, then practise virtue."*
> Greek saying

Your Company's Strengths, Weaknesses, Opportunities and Threats (SWOT) Analysis

Use this analysis every three months to see how you are progressing in general terms. Frequent use means that you can track your growth, and control and correct your failings.

Use the problem-solving analysis for all weaknesses

The good news: when you have identified a weakness, simply go to the problem-solving model at the end of the SWOT analysis and use it to define what caused the problem and how to fix it. Then make sure it is fixed.

Start your SWOT here and answer True or Not True

(If it is true, it is a problem and needs fixing, if it is not true then it is a benefit and needs nurturing)

As Sir Ian MacLennan of BHP in Australia said, "A good mine is one that produces in spite of itself, and the same is true for businesses worldwide." SWOT analyses are like family analyses: we realise we have problems yet we get on okay in spite of them. But fixing the worst bits is a good idea.

Your company's SWOT analysis (Strengths, Weaknesses, Opportunities and Threats)

One: The outside world and you

Changes are happening outside that pose various threats to us.

True   Not True

Whether you answer "True" or "Not true", write in your overall thoughts as to what those threats mean to you, in the space below:

....

....

....

And now analyse what the above means to you via the following SWOT spaces.

S. What are your perceived **Strengths** from the above issue?

....

....

W. What are your perceived **Weaknesses** from the above issue?

....

....

O. What are the **Opportunities** relative to the above issue?

....

....

T. What are the **Threats** relative to the above issue?

....

....

Two: Culture (the internal beliefs and processes of your company)

Note that this section is a reflection only, a reflection of the strategic and tactical direction of the company, up to and including today. Hence we do NOT analyse the strengths, weaknesses, opportunities and threats here; that analysis belongs in the Strategic and Tactical sections that follow further on. When we identify a weakness within the following Strategic and Tactical sections, we need only reverse the behaviour or fix the problem for the culture to change.

Continue to mark True or Not True to all the following

a. The future:

We are not very optimistic about the future True Not True

b. In our work day it seems that:

1.	We are short-term-oriented in our behaviour	True	Not True
2.	We react to circumstances rather than trying to foresee and control them	True	Not True
3.	We seem to be solving past problems more than getting on with current and future client needs	True	Not True

c. Getting things done:

1.	Too much paperwork and too many procedures	True	Not True
2.	And too many managers, not enough action	True	Not True

d. Growing as people:

1.	We don't feel that we are being challenged to do our best	True	Not True
2.	We don't really stretch ourselves to achieve the company's goals as we know them	True	Not True

e. Staff interaction and performance:

1.	It seems to be more important to be popular than to achieve results	True	Not True
2.	We accept anything that is reasonably okay	True	Not True
3.	Risk taking is not encouraged	True	Not True
4.	Creativity is not encouraged	True	Not True
5.	We are not encouraged to try new things, even if we make mistakes	True	Not True

f. Senior management support:

1.	Key managers are not able to support change	True	Not True

g: Internal self-management:

1.	We don't discuss the really difficult issues	True	Not True
2.	Too many excuses, not enough action	True	Not True

3. Problems remain unsolved because we don't speak out or fix them when we do speak out — True — Not True
4. We don't respect each other enough — True — Not True

h. As a result there can be:

1. Face-to-face arguments — True — Not True
2. Behind-their-back remarks of an unkind nature — True — Not True
3. Too much time fighting/blaming one another — True — Not True

i. In teamwork we believe there is:

1. Insufficient teamwork between top and middle management — True — Not True
2. And departments argue against departments resulting in a we/they attitude — True — Not True

Now for your key strategic issues:
(This is where we find out the influences that are shaping our culture, and what we need to reverse or change to improve the way our business operates. Here is where you do your analysis, using the SWOT spaces below.)

Three: Looking at leadership

1. Management is not in control of the organisation — True — Not True
2. Management seeks growth at the expense of profit — True — Not True
3. Management seeks sales at the expense of profit — True — Not True
4. Targets are set that we don't feel we can achieve — True — Not True
5. Everything is urgent and has to be done now — True — Not True
6. We are doing too many different things at the same time — True — Not True
7. We are not sure what the company's goals are — True — Not True

Now analyse your findings via this SWOT section.

Note: Your **strengths** will be those that you marked as **"Not True"** and your **weaknesses** those you marked as **"True"**. **Opportunities** will be those that you now see from your answers, as will **Threats.**

S ....

....

....

W ....

....

....

O ....

....

....

T ....

....

....

Four: How you see your company as being structured

1.	The way the business is organised does not help us meet our goals	True	Not True
2.	People are more important than the goals set	True	Not True
3.	One or two key people make the big decisions	True	Not True
4.	We are not involved in the future plans and decisions	True	Not True
5.	Too many unproductive meetings	True	Not True
6.	Too much management by committee	True	Not True
7.	We are not asked to voice problems, concerns and opinions	True	Not True
8.	We do not develop enough new ideas for our clients and prospects	True	Not True

Your analysis from your answers above:

S ....

....

....

W ....

....

....

O ....

....

....

T ....

....

....

Five: The way we are rewarded

The way we are paid does not encourage us to reach the company's goals True Not True

Your analysis from your answer above:

S ....

....

....

W ....

....

....

O ....

....

....

T ....

....

....

Now for your key tactical issues:
Here we learn even more about the behaviour of your company and what you need to change or reverse to be more successful—thereby changing the culture of the company.

More analysis is required using the SWOT spaces at the end of each section.

Six: You and your competition, customers and prospects

1.	We don't worry enough about our competition	True	Not true
2.	We are at the mercy of our systems rather than market driven	True	Not True
3.	We are not really focused on client satisfaction	True	Not True
4.	We are not trained to know how our performance affects the customer's sense of quality and satisfaction	True	Not True
5.	We do not have clear definitions of customer-defined quality and service	True	Not True

Your analysis from your answers above:

S ....

....

....

W ....

....

....

O ....

....

....

T ....

....

....

Seven: Your business, its tactics

1.	We rely on too few key customers	True	Not True
2.	We do not understand our marketing plan	True	Not True
3.	We do not know if we are correctly positioned in our market	True	Not True
4.	Our prices/fees are too high compared to our competition	True	Not True
5.	We do not adequately promote our business and all that it offers	True	Not True
6.	We are not satisfied with our corporate image and identity	True	Not True

Your analysis from your answers above:

S ....

....

....

W ....

....

....

O ....

....

....

T ....

....

....

Eight: Space to work in, equipment and systems to work with

1.	We are growing too fast for our space	True	Not True
2.	We struggle with outdated technology	True	Not True
3.	We have too many procedures and policies	True	Not True
4.	We don't follow our procedures and policies	True	Not True
5.	Our workflow could be more efficient	True	Not True

6. Our accounting systems could be more efficient — True — Not True

Your analysis from your answers above:

S ....

....

....

W ....

....

....

O ....

....

....

T ....

....

....

Nine: People, hiring, evaluating, training

1. We are short-staffed most of the time — True — Not True
2. We are not good at selecting effective people — True — Not True
3. You can get away with being incompetent — True — Not True
4. Performance is rarely if ever evaluated effectively — True — Not True
5. We keep low-performing people on, rather than make waves — True — Not True
6. People have to learn as they go, without proper induction and training — True — Not True
7. We do not have a sense of being developed for management or other career paths — True — Not True
8. Management can't cope with the current demands of the job — True — Not True
9. Too many people are not contributing — True — Not True
10. Too many people are in the wrong jobs — True — Not True

11. We are missing some supervisory and management skills in key positions True Not True

Your analysis from your answers above:

S ....

....

....

W ....

....

....

O ....

....

....

T ....

....

....

Ten: At the end of the day

(This is where we get an overall picture of your company. On the way through the earlier statements, it may have seemed that there are a lot of difficult issues. This section, however, may point up only a few key issues after all.)

1. We sometimes make too many mistakes True Not True
2. We are up and down in our relationships internally and with clients True Not True
3. We achieve little in real terms on a daily basis True Not True
4. We have low morale True Not True
5. Some of our staff are burnt out True Not True
6. Some of our customers complain too much True Not True
7. Other similar businesses are more competitive than we are True Not True
8. Our financial management is inadequate True Not True

9. We lose too many valued clients	True	Not true
10. We lose too many clients overall	True	Not True
11. We don't know why we lose clients	True	Not True
12. We don't get enough new clients	True	Not True
13. Our clients seem bored with our product/service	True	Not True
14. We market inefficiently and without consistency	True	Not True

Now write in your key issues from this analysis (the Strategic sections 3–5 and the Tactical sections 6–9, nominating those which your "gut feeling" tells you are the most important.

Strengths
Strategic: go to your notes in sections 3–5 and choose those issues of key importance. (Remember that these strategic strengths will always be found in the statements marked "Not True.")

....

....

....

Strengths
Tactical: go to sections 6–9 and choose those issues of key importance. (Remember that these tactical strengths will always be found in the statements marked "Not True.")

....

....

....

Weaknesses
Strategic: go to your notes in sections 3–5 and choose those issues of key importance. (Remember that these strategic weaknesses will always be found in the statements marked "True.")

....

....

....

Weaknesses

Tactical: go back to sections 6–9 and choose those issues of key importance. (Remember that these tactical weaknesses will always be found in the statements marked "True.")

....

....

....

Opportunities

Strategic: go back again to sections 3–5. Go back through your notes in the SWOT analysis and define those opportunities of key importance.

....

....

....

Opportunities

Tactical: go back again to sections 6–9. Go back through your notes in the SWOT analysis and define those opportunities of key importance.

....

....

....

Threats

Strategic: return once more to sections 3–5. Go back through your notes in the SWOT analysis and define those issues of key importance, by your gut feel.

....

....

....

Threats

Tactical: return once more to sections 6–9. Go back through your notes in the SWOT analysis and define those issues of key importance, by your gut feel.

....

....

....

At the end of the day

Nominate your key issues from section 10, working on your gut feeling.

Strengths (from "Not True")

....

....

....

Weaknesses (from "True")

....

....

....

Opportunities (from those decided on by gut feeling from your notes)

....

....

....

Threats (from those decided on by gut feeling from your notes)

....

....

....

Combine your findings in a report on your overall strengths, weaknesses, opportunities and threats and use the following problem-solving model for any and every problem you may have, be it personal or business. Repeat this process every three months and note your progress.

Now for the problem solving of your weaknesses

Disregard for the moment the weaknesses from the "culture" section, as culture is only a reflection of the strategic and tactical direction imposed on the business, up to and including today.

Instead look at the weaknesses in the strategic and tactical sections and work on those. The culture of your business will change as the weaknesses are reversed.

Here is the problem-solving model to help you make those changes.

This exercise works well with a partner similarly involved in the business. Hence I have nominated an A and a B. But you can do it on your own if you have no likely person to work with you.

B asks you, A, the following set of questions and writes down the response.

1. What is the problem? (If from the SWOT analysis write in the exact words, or the way you have redefined it.)

   ....

   ....

   ....

2. What caused the problem?

   ....

   ....

   ....

3. How is this limiting you?

   ....

   ....

   ....

4. What are the long-term consequences of this situation if it continues?

   ....

   ....

   ....

5. Is this a recurring problem?

....

....

....

B now asks A the following set of questions and writes in the response.

1. What are three possible solutions?

   a ....

   b ....

   c ....

2. Which of these do you prefer?

....

....

....

....

3. What will that do for you?

....

....

....

4. How can you make it happen for you?

....

....

....

5. How can you use this obstacle to become more successful?

....

....

....

6. How will this experience benefit you in the future?

....

....

....

Now take whatever action is needed to ensure a result, which includes developing a working party of no more than eight people, and preferably fewer, to truly identify the levels of the problem, and how best to fix it.

> *"Nothing succeeds like the appearance of success."*
> Christopher Lascl

Step 1: Part B

Powerful Business and Marketing Plan

Now that you have done your business SWOT analysis, you are ready for your strategic and tactical business plan:

Key issue: There are three "musts" to having a successful company. You must have

- Good product
- Good marketing and
- Good financial management.

If any one of these three is missing, your business will fail. Please first read through this whole section before doing any planning, so that you get a clear understanding of what planning is all about and why you are doing it.

Be realistic, congruent and relevant

> *"Miss a meal but never miss a good book."* Jim Rohn

In item 2 of the business plan (p. 54) we will ask, "What do I want for my business by the future date that I am looking back from?" Say you are a company making children's toys.

It is important to put your wants into a congruent flow so that each enhances the other. For instance, you want to increase profit by fifteen per cent per annum over the next three years. You can do it by either cutting costs or expanding your sales profitably.

Let's say you choose to cut costs by cutting back staffing, year one. However, you want to increase your Research & Development division so that you will be prepared for the next toy-selling season. And you want to improve customer service and production quality because your research shows you're seen as unhelpful with complaints—of which you have too many.

Now you have two plans which call for increased staff and facilities, pulling against the plan to cut staff. Your decision to increase profit by fifteen per cent will die on the vine. Let's say you decide to expand profitably instead.

If you are absolute market leader in your field, you are the benchmark for all other similar companies. If, however, you are below that first position, your key question is: where do you now lie, relative to your competition? You need to know in order to verify your belief that you can achieve an increase of fifteen per cent over the years of your business plan.

First work out the industry norm for increase in sales. Look at total sales of all similar companies (adjusted for inflation) over the past three years. Did you increase your sales more/less/the same in comparison? If more, was it sufficient to make you feel secure about achieving your fifteen per cent increase?

If the industry norm has been a ten per cent increase over the past few years and you have achieved that also, there is not a great deal of reason to think you can reach an increase of fifteen per cent without considerable expenditure of (for example) time and money in customer service, staff training and better product, sales force, packaging, response time, distribution, advertising and promotional activities, plus tighter financial controls.

If, however, you find an industry norm of fifteen per cent and you have not achieved it, it is time to look at why, before you make any plans for the future.

> *"I don't make jokes. I just watch the government and report the facts."* Will Rogers (1879–1935)

It can be that you used to achieve industry norm or even beyond in growth, but you have changed as an organisation and have moved from a shooting star, high in activity, excitement and low in cash, to a sort of middle-aged spread where you have no real competitive advantage any more, you are just one of many struggling to make a living.

In that case you have to find a whole new way of looking at your business plan. What is it that you want for your company relative to the truth as you now see it? Could you occupy a niche supplying educational toys by catalogue to parents anxious to entertain and educate their children other than with TV?

How would this impact on your current systems? Could it be done cost-effectively or would you go broke in making all the changes long before the product had a chance of making money?

Who is your purchaser?

> *"Almost anything is easier to get into than to get out of."*
> Allen's Law

Key issue:
After people see something they like, they buy from greed, fear and laziness. Are you meeting all three in your selling process?

Another good question is: does anyone really want my product? Is there so much competition around that people buy what they see, rather than by brand?

Will your product be overtaken by cheaper overseas imports? Could you manufacture overseas and distribute from there more cheaply and effectively, thereby ridding yourself of the complaints problem? That could be good news.

If the industry norm is ten per cent growth and you have achieved that plus a twelve per cent or thirteen per cent profit increase in the past three years, you may achieve your fifteen per cent profit increase, all things being equal, even while improving your customer service and Research and Development. Go for it . . . but with caution.

What is your market share? A simple mathematical process will tell you. You divide your annual sales by that of the total industry sales of similar companies. If you sold $1000 of toys and the total industry sales were $1,000,000 you would have 0.001% market share (according to my calculator).

Your relative market share is also interesting. To find this out you divide your sales for the year by that of your nearest competitor. If you did $1000 and they did $2000, your relative market share is 50%; if they did only $1500 it is 66%. Have you been growing faster than your competitor or falling behind?

> *"The enemy came. He was beaten. I am tired. Goodnight."*
> Message sent by Vicomte Turenne after the battle of Dunen, 1658

If you are a service organisation, ask yourself—does your marketplace really need another recruitment company, another firm of management consultants, another accounting or law firm, another travel agent, another restaurant? What is their industry norm for sales growth over the past three years? Where do you stand? How can you differentiate yourself and what therefore should be your approach to your business plan?

Since you can only grow by taking on more clients and customers or more business from existing clients (and if you do not grow, you go backwards), then your business plan must be about increasing staff and facilities in order to increase business and taking a realistic approach to recouping those costs. Clients and prospects do not read your business plans, they simply do what they want, when they want.

Where do you need to be in the future?

> *"Technology is dominated by two types of people: those who understand what they do not manage, and those who manage what they do not understand."* Putt's Law

Item 3 being land, labour and capital, where do you need to be in the future on these three subjects? That question will be answered when you define the business plan for item 2. If you decide to contract or expand your staffing you may want to create a small, efficient task force to move you out of where you are now to where you want to be in the time scale you have chosen.

Your present staff may change in numbers and/or in style and qualifications. An accounting firm that decides to focus on an ethnic group rather than take on all comers may seek people of that race or nationality to work with clients.

A legal firm specialising in immigration from third-world countries may seek people who have spent time in these areas.

A management consultancy may decide to focus on the tourist industry and hire people from airlines, hotels, shipping lines and travel agencies.

All the while it must be acknowledged that the return on the investment will take a long time coming. Which brings us to capital. Realistically, how much money will you need for these changes to take place and return a profit? Over years of doing budgets where many variables are involved, I have found one unchanging rule: whatever budget you set, it always costs twice as much. This seems to apply to personal budgets as well as business ones. The key question is, can you afford the plans you have for the future?

Research your existing client base

> *"If you cannot convince them, confuse them."*
>
> Truman's Law

Item 4 requires you to research your existing client base and ask what they think of your organisation, what they consider you provide and how they think you can adapt or grow for the future.

One of the world's favourite stories is about the railroad companies that thought they ran trains up and down lines. To the rest of the world they provided a mode of transport. While the train companies stuck to their knitting (so to speak), other transport opportunities passed them by, as did their passengers.

You need to know whether your clients love you or are staying with you until a better offer comes along. Clients are fickle and will move for almost any reason, including a better price.

For instance, I ran a very successful series of travel supplements in all the major newspapers with free gifts and prizes and great holiday offers from Thomas Cook. The day that promotion finished, another travel company came out with some more good offers. My client's outlets emptied as the others filled.

Absolutely no loyalty! But why should there be when almost all travel shops provide the same range of products? The same is true of a lot of other companies.

The changing needs of your clients and how you respond to

them can have a lot to do with government legislation and regulations.

If the client cannot understand the new rules on superannuation, for instance, and you can, you have a captive market—but only if you can explain it in a way that we confused buyers can understand. Otherwise, we still feel doubtful and confused. And no-one makes a major purchase decision feeling like that.

You now know about your sales volume, growth rate and market share at this time and have thought about what these must be to meet your future plans. "Adapt or die" is a fair statement at this stage because whatever your expansion plans, you have to have the systems, processes and trained people to make them happen.

Recently I talked with a large retailer about a test market for data collection and lifestyle marketing programs. In conversation with the MIS department I found they are well set up to handle the information flow except that they are also on an acquisition program and about the time the test would be ready to go national, they may well have run out of spare mainframe capacity.

We started out talking about the business plan for introducing database marketing; now we were talking about major costs in systems. Will the database marketing program return sufficient funds to cover these costs in 2, 3, 5 years or never? Will the company want to take that risk along with the cost of the acquisitions?

Action and reaction. However realistic and congruent your plans are, you have to have the people, processes, systems and training to make it work, as well as the capital.

How well is your product or service promoted?

> *"He who hesitates is probably right."* Bogovich's Law

Item 5 asks how well your product or service is promoted to the buying public. First of all, do you have a "single-minded proposition" which quite simply states what you provide from the customer's point of view?

(This subject of the single-minded proposition is covered more fully in Step Five.)

For instance in one case we thought of a timber and hardware company as being "doctors" to the building and DIY trade, prescribing the best products for the job at hand. If proven, this could then translate to a tag line, "Building better communities with care".

This kind of tag line, while not researched and given here as a discussion point only, does show how all their communications—to the trade or the consumer, in direct marketing, sales promotion, catalogue sales or public relations—could have a single-minded focus, simply because that one statement was the umbrella under which everything else could hang.

Item 5 therefore depends, in my opinion, on your finding the right, researched answer to the question of your "single-minded" proposition. Twelve words or less is a great discipline.

When you come up with that statement and use it to create a tag line for all your communications, you can then decide whether or not you have top-quality advertising, sales promotion, direct marketing, public relations and community relations by comparing your profit pre and post the use of this discipline.

There will be many other factors that affect your profit, but having clear, simple-minded communications takes you way out in front of the muddled ways of most of your competitors.

Care for the environment

> *"Any simple idea will be worded in the most complicated way."*
> Malek's Law

Item 6 is community affairs. The section that asks, "Am I contributing to the environment or taking away?" is one of the most critical in our plans for the coming decades.

Recent research shows that at the top of people's concerns are unemployment and the environment, nominated by around seventy per cent of people interviewed. All other issues were around twenty per cent.

So what do we care about in corporate life? We care about the environment because, if we don't, we may well be boycotted out of business.

People rightly believe that the world is running out of the

capacity to heal itself, while we humans do not have the capacity to adapt well to increasing pollution. So we have to solve the problem. In your business plan look very carefully at this responsibility even if it seems at first that you can't do much.

If everyone cleaned up their back and front yards for instance, we would clean up the world. Think of the miracle of the Sydney Harbour clean-up. It led to "Clean Up Australia" and beyond to the world level. It can be done. It should—it must—be part of everyone's plan for the future.

> *"Orthodox medicine has not found an answer to your complaint. However, luckily for you, I happen to be a quack."*
> Richter cartoon caption

We want healthy people in our communities who will need our products and services. Sick people have entirely different needs and most of us are not basing our future on being part of the hospital and medical professions. If we make the difference now, we will have clients for the future.

Other government legislation on equal opportunity, sexual harassment, smoking in the workplace/staff health care/the rights of part-time workers and superannuation requires specialist knowledge. Seek it out, get different opinions, attend seminars and make judgments based on sound information.

Training is important and probably the greatest problem faced by corporations today is how to evaluate programs and their effectiveness.

Training organisations all over the world have public seminars so that one or two people can attend before you decide to have a specially focused in-house program. Their trainers are rated after every "performance" and any bad rating is discussed. Therefore only the good ones survive.

Evaluating effectiveness after training can be as simple as deciding what needs to be fixed, getting it fixed and then seeing if it remains fixed. In my experience, our peer group and immediate managers are the best judges of whether our improvement is ongoing.

> *"Money oils the wheels of choice."* Anon

Your vision for the future

> *"No matter what goes wrong, it will probably look right."*
> Scott's First Law

And now for a vision statement, as in item 7. I remember sitting in Procter & Gamble's office in Hong Kong reading their vision statement, which included giving people the right environment to grow in, to express truth fearlessly, to stand up for what is right and to expect a fair hearing for their opinions, while producing the finest quality products for their customers.

The meeting progressed entirely along those lines. We expected and received a fair hearing for our opinions. As for their products, P & G does have an awesome reputation for product purity. Their vision statement represented their attitude to their customers and to their staff.

Your vision statement should be broad enough to allow for expansion and precise enough for all staff members to feel that they can be part of it.

It is fair to say that if the staff have a say in the vision statement and the business plan, you will get more realistic and congruent objectives than you could achieve in isolation or in a small ivory-tower group.

Say you were a restaurant owner and you chose six to eight words or phrases to describe your business, now and for the future. You might have noticed that you have, and want to continue to have, "friendly staff, fair prices, great service, great food, clean workplace".

Then your vision statement in terms of what you plan to do for your customers might become: "We provide and will continue to provide fine quality food at very fair prices, having constant regard for the highest standards of service and cleanliness and concern for the environment."

> *"I've known what it is to be hungry, but I always went right to a restaurant."* Ring Lardner (1885–1993)

This could mean that you serve only fresh seasonal foods to get the highest quality and the fairest prices, that your staff are hired away from the best hotels and that they and your kitchen are scrubbed pristine clean.

You also use biodegradable washing powders and recycled paper products if you are convinced that the chemicals in recycling do less harm than chopping down renewable trees.

"Providing food" is broad enough to allow for expansion into boardroom catering, special event catering, airport and airline food, staff cafeterias for major business buildings and meals for workers on special projects.

You could go on to children's parties and theme restaurants such as great eateries for truck drivers . . . the list is endless. The choice is yours because your vision is focused but flexible.

> *"When an error has been detected and corrected, it will be found to have been correct in the first place."*
>
> Scott's Second Law

Now for your business plan

To begin your strategic business plan ask yourself what is a truly relevant date to plan towards.

Your product cycle may be such that three years is a relevant business plan analysis for you. Five, ten or fifteen years may be better if you are building fleets of container ships or satellites, all the while remembering that constant revision of your business plan is necessary.

Choose a future point in time that is really valid for you, stand there, look back to today and fill in the following details.

1. What is my business about today? (Write today's date in here .../.../....... and describe your business now.)

   ....

   ....

   ....

   ....

   ....

   ....

2. Stand in the future and look back to today and ask, "What do I want for my business by the future date that I am looking back from?" (Write that future date in here .../.../...... and describe those developments.)

....

....

....

....

....

....

3. How do we get from the present to the future? In its barest bones a business plan has three elements: land, labour and capital. The next step is to analyse these three:
   a. Where is my business physically situated now?

   ....

   ....

   b. Where should it be in this future time?

   ....

   ....

   c. Who do I have working with me now?

   ....

   ....

   d. How would this change for the future?

   ....

   ....

   e. How am I doing for money now?

   ....

   ....

   f. How much will I need to get to the future?

   ....

   ....

4. The next key issue is developing your product or service through understanding the customers' needs:

What am I producing now?

5. What do my clients think of this product/service?

....

....

....

....

6. How must I improve the product/service and its production to still be in business by my chosen time?

....

....

....

....

7. What is my sales volume/growth rate/market share now?

....

....

....

8. What must my sales volume/growth rate/market share be in this forward time to cover all expenses and make a satisfactory profit which allows for reinvestment, product improvement, price reduction, or greater spending on advertising and promotion? (Otherwise a better and cheaper competitor is likely to come into your market.)

....

....

....

....

9. What systems, processes, special training must I put in place to reach that objective?

....

....

....

....

10. And next, how well is my product/service promoted to the buying market?

 How well do I express in my sales/marketing and advertising activities what it is that is unique about my product?

 ....

 ....

 ....

 (Write in here your "single-minded" proposition—see Step Five. Try to do it in twelve words or less.) Now write down an appropriate tag line that would follow from the single-minded proposition (see relevant chapter).

 ....

 ....

 ....

 ....

11. Am I now doing top-quality:

Client/prospect relations?	Yes	No
Advertising?	Yes	No
Direct marketing?	Yes	No
Sales promotion?	Yes	No
Public relations?	Yes	No
Staff relations?	Yes	No
Community relations?	Yes	No

 Your comments.

 ....

 ....

 ....

12. In making decisions about your advertising and promotion, the following received wisdoms are here to assist you in allocating your money and activities. As you promote your products, you will find that different media give different results, such as:

 • Radio advertising brings in brand-new customers; print and TV advertising help move clients and customers from your competition; direct marketing builds customer loyalty.

Plus:

- You have to spend money in order to be noticed. About half of what you spend will keep you "top of mind" with your existing client base, the other half will attract new purchasers.
- Shout, don't whisper. One small advertisement will be lost in the clutter, whereas one big one or twelve little ones, page by page, will call out loudly for attention.
- The big spend comes first. When you have cut through the clutter of your competitors' advertising and promotional activities, you can reduce your spending considerably, to one-quarter or one-half.
- Use more than one medium at a time. Print or TV plus radio will return you up to fifty per cent more responses when they are used together rather than separately.
- Don't struggle for the perfect advertising campaign at the expense of missing your deadline. Good is better, but getting out there is best.
- Most of all, it doesn't matter what you do so long as you get out there and do something. If you smile in the dark, no-one can see you. If you smile in the light, the world can smile with you. Don't sit behind closed doors, fearing failure and rejection. Get out there and do something that people can notice and respond to.
- Above all, be different from your competition. If you match their advertising expenditure and use the same media, have the same special offers, look the same, sound the same, you will disappear into their image, not create your own.

Ask yourself—using these guidelines—how should I improve/expand these communication processes to meet my future goals?

....

....

....

....

....

....

....

13. Community affairs are also a key issue, such as, am I contributing to the earth's environment or taking away?

....

....

....

....

....

And—what must I do to be ready for/ahead of government legislation on this and other issues such as equal opportunity/sexual harassment*/smoking in the workplace and staff healthcare/superannuation/paternity leave and maternity leave/training levy, etc.?

• The best and simplest guideline I have come across for staff on the sexual harassment issue is this: ask yourself if you would like to:

(a) Hear your words repeated on radio;
(b) See your actions replayed on television;
(c) Have your family walk in on you at this time;
(d) Behave the same way in a place of worship.

If the answer is "No!" to any of these questions, then it is sexual harassment.

14. Training for now and the future: are my staff trained in a planned and coordinated way that is relevant to their and my needs? Or is the training largely haphazard? Or non-existent?

....

....

....

....

What must I therefore put in place to guarantee the training which is required for my future plans to work?

....

....

....

....

15. Now comes a simple vision statement for the future as to what you plan to provide to the client or customer and how well you are going to do it. First write down about six words that describe your service or product now and then as you want it to be in the future for your staff and clients/customers.

....

....

Next put those words together in a sentence that is clear to you, your staff and the people who buy from you.

....

....

....

Publish thousands of cards with that vision statement on it. Ask your clients/customers to mark "yes" or "no" beside the question, "Did we match our vision statement in our relationship with you?"

Use these cards as market research. Ask for the client's name and phone number on the card and contact each one to ask what was good or not good about your relationship. Learn how to do better as you go—before it is too late.

It may be timely here to mention the definition of quality service: it is simply doing what you say you will do, within the time stated.

Key issue: there are only three ways to grow your company. Grow your client base, grow your profit, grow the frequency of purchase. Are you skilled up to do all three?

Now that your business plan is complete, move on to your marketing plan.

Outline of your marketing plan

> *"They say you can't do it, but sometimes it doesn't always work."* Casey Stengel (1891–1975)

When you have completed your business plan, you will need a marketing plan to follow, for the development of sales of your products or services.

I am delighted to recommend to you the following marketing plan revised from *Marketing Without Mystery—a Practical Guide to Writing a Marketing Plan,* Amacom, 1991 by Laura M. Dirks and Sally H. Daniels. (Buy this book, it is stunning.)

Start first with:

1. Background and objectives:
   - A brief statement of background information about your company and what you provide.

     ....

     ....

     ....
   - The reasons you are writing this plan and the period of time that it will cover.

     ....

     ....

     ....
   - The specific maximum and minimum objectives of the plan (so that you can measure success as you go along).

     ....

     ....

     ....
   - An agreed vision statement as to what you will provide your customers and staff during the period of this marketing plan.

     ....

     ....

     ....
2. Who your likely buyers are:
   - A brief description of the people/companies that will buy from you.

     ....

     ....

     ....

- Their needs that your product/service and this plan will serve.

  ....

  ....

  ....

  ....

3. Who the competition is and how well it performs:

   ....

   ....

   ....

   ....

   An evaluation of who your competition is, both directly

   ....

   ....

   ....

   And indirectly.

   ....

   ....

   ....

   For instance, a travel company may have a direct competitor next door but all other phone booking processes are an indirect competitor, because your clients can book direct and bypass you.

   - How well that direct and indirect competition serves (or otherwise) this market.

     ....

     ....

     ....

   - How your direct competition may react to your plans.

     ....

     ....

     ....

- How your indirect competition will react.

    ....

    ....

    ....

4. Promotional activities that you plan to use such as:
    - Publicity/PR—if you do not have the skills in-house, hire a good PR firm.

        ....

        ....

        ....

    - Direct/database marketing—again, hire a good firm if you do not have the skills.

        ....

        ....

        ....

    - Advertising: go with the best advertising agency you can find. They all charge about the same! Remember, a great client makes a great agency, not the other way round.

        Make your advertising agency your business partner. Be there for brainstorming sessions, help them see the whole picture by sharing your goals, your business plans, your marketing plans, your results. Like doctors, they can't help you effectively until they know the whole picture.

        ....

        ....

        ....

        ....

    - Personal selling: what this book is all about. Stay within the three-month cycle. Make contact regularly and relentlessly and never fail to follow up.

        ....

        ....

        ....

- Telemarketing for appointments or sale of your product, with a free-phone response number.

  ....

  ....

  ....

- Special events in the areas where your likely buyers can most easily respond.

  ....

  ....

  ....

- Mobile offices for these special events.

  ....

  ....

  ....

Step 2

A wide band of well-chosen prospects

> *"When all is said and done, more is said than done."*
> Unknown

Over twenty-five years ago, when the Saatchi brothers first set up shop in London, they had a staff of twelve. Two people managed new-business development; the other ten administered the advertising process.

One day, Saatchi's David Miln was pondering the problem of how to drum up new business. He remembered a geography lesson from his youth in England when he had learned about the old English canal system for moving product to distribution and manufacturing sites.

In those old days, before the invention of the engine, horses pulled barges down the canals. Tied by ropes to the barges, the horses walked down paths on the canals' banks. Nudged and encouraged by their drivers, they pulled the barge through the canals and the locks, down the waterways to the factory.

David recalled his teacher saying that if the horses were nudged gently, each in their turn, the first barge eventually arrived at the factory, followed by the second and third and so on. As each barge was unloaded at the pier, the horse and barge were put back into the system and, one day, each came around again.

David began to realise that if you're going to be in business for a long time, you have to have a whole lot of barges (prospects) being gently and regularly nudged down the waterways into your business. If you stop gentling the barges through the waterways, eventually the vessels will stop and there will be no barges arriving at your factory.

Push the barges (prospects) regularly down the canal (meaning roadway to your business)

> *"A good man is always a beginner."* Martial (c.40–c.104)

Let's say you own a cornflake factory. A ship comes into port full of fresh corn, but your factory is at a far distant point along a series of canals. By off-loading the corn onto barges, and pushing those barges along the canal at regular intervals, the first one will arrive, in due course, at the factory.

Then, kept in motion by a consistent process, golden corn will turn up regularly and relentlessly at your cornflake factory. If a barge comes by with corn that is not the right quality for your factory, you can let it go, because there are always more coming.

The cornflake factory story is the same for any business. A wide band of prospects, nudged regularly and relentlessly, will one day tip gold into your company's bank account.

No longer choke the life out of too few prospects, but build relationships with many

> *"Women speak two languages, one of which is verbal."*
> Steve Rubenstein

Throughout my working life I have been struck by how similar business is to our personal lives. You can wreck it or build it depending on your attitude and behaviour. The nudging process of business development is much the same as the way we look after our relationships with people we care about.

Unbidden, we will think of them and ask them to lunch, or take an extra cup of coffee in to talk over a problem. We will send a memo or a fax as an update on something of importance to them.

We might send them a magazine cutting. Meet them at an

airport. Buy them a book we found of value. Send a postcard. Remember their birthday. Invite them to our Christmas or New Year party. Without quite knowing how, we have stayed in touch because it is easy, pleasant and rewarding.

You need do no more in your nudging of prospects. It is not hard to have lunch with someone you have grown to like. It is nice to come by for coffee, having first checked to see if it suits. You can pass on an opinion about a movie they have expressed an interest in.

Sharing magazine articles is a very kind gesture in an overloaded world, as are newspaper clippings from editions outside the usual. Postcards from abroad please the whole office, especially if you're having a terrible time in a typhoon.

Remembering birthdays is a knockout and even more fun is to research the foundation date of the company and send a cake for the company's birthday.

The effect is highly impressive and I once won a conference and dinner at the Auckland Inter-Continental hotel for many hundreds of people doing just that a year in advance of the company's one hundred year anniversary.

I sent a cake and a letter saying: "On this day next year you will be celebrating your one hundredth anniversary and we would be delighted to be the venue of choice."

The bonus was that the company had no idea until then that it was their centenary, so were delighted to have a year up their sleeves to plan for it. And yes, we took the booking on the spot! Nudging a wide band of well-chosen prospects is fun, it's creative, it's rewarding and it makes a lot of people happy, including you.

So how wide is that band? In Hong Kong we had one hundred thousand names on our database.

That regular, relentless, without-fail contacting every three months increased our market share of disposable diapers from 13% to 42%—and each point was worth US$1,000,000 over the life usage of the product. We would have had 55% market share but the product got hijacked and sold in Taiwan instead. (Yes, we were upset about that.)

At Thomas Cook's we had over 60,000 leisure travellers "captured" by 20 or more parameters. In London we had 400 companies that I was pursuing. In New York it was 8,000 across America. It is amazing what you can do with computer-generated mailings and follow-up phone calls.

It is also amazing how little following up people do. All over the world I ask people to raise their hands if they have ever had a **second** call from a sales person to whom they first said "No". And all over the world I get the same response: very few hands showing, or none at all.

Then I ask, "Keep your hand up if you ever had a **third** call from a sales person to whom you first said 'No'." Every hand is down. It is that easy to be different. You just have to keep calling back, and being creatively interesting in your follow-up activities.

My favourite is to send in a breakfast basket of croissant, orange juice, marmalade, butter and a small knife with a note saying, "My ideas are as fresh and as classical as the breakfast I send you". I sign the note "W".

Later that day I send in my book saying, "My ideas are as fresh and as classical as the breakfast I sent you today. I will call you for an appointment. Enjoy!" And I sign the card and the book in full. Yes, I do get an appointment every time.

I was talking a few days ago with a salesperson who had been in that "contact once and never again" cycle. She had spent two years skimming over the top of people's needs, never once going back to consolidate. She and millions of others of people involved in sales do that. Why, I know not.

Recently I rang, faxed and wrote to a prospect. He rang me back and said crossly, "Why are you contacting me endlessly?" And I said, "To prove that what I do works." He laughed and said, "You're right, come on in."

My favourite story is about a New York friend, Barbara Rogers. She rang me and asked if I had told Jim Johnson to call her. I said, "No—who is Jim Johnson?"

"Well," she said, "he rang me and said, oh so nicely, that he was sure I was happy with my current accountant but if not, he would like to take that role. I replied that I was well looked after and he then said, 'Thank you, Mrs Rogers, and if I may, I will call you back on Monday in four weeks time at 3 pm, just to check.'"

And he did, on the dot. And he got the job. Why? Because as Barbara said, he was the only person who had **ever** called her twice, let alone on the dot of the day and time stated. She said, "If he runs his business as well as this, imagine what he could do for mine."

Simple, yes?

Key points to remember

- You need to have a wide band of well-chosen prospects.
- You must nudge them regularly and relentlessly, caringly and creatively. Never let them go.

But where do we find good new prospects? The next step will help you.

Step Three

Define your prospect base using the Commonality Survey

> *"Good judgment comes from experience and experience comes from bad judgment."* Barry LePatner

Choosing your prospects well can seem a very hard task. You stand at the window, looking out over the mass of people in streets, offices, parks, buses and cars, and think, "How will I ever find my likely prospects?" Help is at hand in this step.

First, before going ahead with your Commonality Survey, pause to consider who your competitors are. Is your product or service better, more efficient, cheaper/better value for money, more accessible than theirs?

If yes, you can readily win over their type of good client. If no, then fix things now! Your success will depend heavily on finding those people who are not (but could be) your clients/customers, understanding why not, finding out what it is you can do to change that and nudging them regularly and relentlessly into buying from you.

Your best new-client prospects should look like your existing best clients and the best clients of your competition. In researching prospective buyers, look for common threads to create your self-answering/self-teaching Client Commonality Survey (in this instance written for companies with a service or product to sell).

Ask yourself:

What is it about your current clients that you like, in terms of their personalities and how they deal with you?

Where are they geographically?

What industries are they in?

How many existing clients are small businesses as defined by the Small Business Association?

How many existing clients are male, how many female; how many children, how many are not of local origin?

What size company are they, based on amount of revenue generated, staff size and ranking in the top one hundred?

What are they buying from you now?

What do these existing clients think of your product?

Talk to them and find out. To do so will enlarge your view of what your new-business marketplace can be. For instance, ask yourself if you may readily attract more minority groups, men, women, children, families, older people.

Get the big picture first. Then ask what *type* of minority group, man, woman, child, family, older person. It can also help you to find that single-minded proposition and that key phrase to describe your product; an invaluable shorthand way for you to present yourself to the world. Which of your existing clients are most profitable? Why are they profitable and how can you use this information to define similar prospects?

Example: a jeweller researched who exactly was contributing to his bottom line. He found that non-whites buying gold gave him 32% of his profit. With this information he reallocated his media spend and lifted that market to 50% of his profit.

And what clients have you lost and why? This is an issue that you will want to face squarely and examine carefully. It is of critical interest to the wellbeing and future growth of your business. It's rare for people to hear what they don't want to hear. Have courage. Ask, listen and learn.

While all of these issues are significant, greater weight might be given to geographical location and the personalities you most enjoy being with.

People tend to do more business with people they can reach easily and whom they like. Moreover, it is likely that there are excellent prospects within your own business district with whom you have never been in touch.

It is interesting that entrepreneurs seeking new business will often travel forty blocks, drive kilometres, jump on a plane, cross rivers and mountains, but will seldom work in their immediate locality, let alone their own office building. All they come back with is huge expense accounts.

Never mistake motion for action.The prospects who are physically nearest can be the richest mine of your life, because you will spend less and get a higher response from them. Find local prospects, contact them until they are ready to become clients and keep them. Remember, it is critical to have a high volume of prospects for success to follow.

Remember too, that people buy from ***greed, fear*** and ***laziness***. Are you meeting all three with your product, service and pricing?

Examples: a recent client told me that she had bought both a house and a car from greed, fear and laziness. Her current house was cold in winter and she couldn't take it one more time. She found a warm, sunny place and bought it because the price was right (greed), the winter would no longer hold such terror for her (fear) and if she closed the deal she could stop looking (laziness).

Similarly with her car. Her previous car was new a year ago, but always breaking down. She saw the car she liked at the right price and "snap!" she bought it. There was greed because the price was right, fear because the other one kept breaking down at all the wrong times (is there ever a right time?) and laziness—now she could get on with earning money and stop wasting time looking.

Another client told me a similar story. He hates buying clothes but his wife rang at work and told him that his favourite store was having a big sale and he was to go! He did and spent a fortune.

Greed was involved because it was 50% off; fear of his wife if he did not buy; and laziness, because if he bought enough for the next ten years he would not have to go back until well into the 21st century!

> *"Charm is a way of getting the answer yes without asking a clear question."* Albert Camus (1913–1960)

All that being said, in the end the ultimate issue in your business building is the people you deal with. As much as they want quality service (and good prices and being rescued from laziness and fear), you want quality communications, respect, integrity and fair dealing. Until you get that you will not be happy.

Again, this is why the broad band of prospects is so important: it gives you space to find the right clients.

Business development is just like your personal life. You keep in touch with your friends, take an interest in their activities, help where you can with advice or actions, send cards, remember special occasions with gifts, do nice things when you can.

Similarly, you know exactly how to lose a relationship. Forget to ring, turn up late, promise but don't deliver, be abrupt when you should be patient, expect more than you are prepared to give. All of this goes on in business and it is easier to lose a client or prospect than it is a long-term friend, who is rather more inclined to forgive and forget.

The exciting next step is to look beyond what is common into creatively relevant possibilities. For instance, Procter & Gamble realised that some elderly people became incontinent, and created an adult product for that market.

Coca-Cola foresaw the move to less sugar and more healthy living, but they launched their Diet Coke quietly until proven. Now it is promoted with great vigour. But when Coca-Cola decided to radically change their core product, the world rebelled, requiring them to backtrack and have Classic Coke as well as the new Coke.

See how your existing products can be modified to meet a market need, rather than create totally new products for which you have no known reputation—and which will cost a great deal of money to promote to a level of profitable acceptance.

In essence it is a matter of keeping core products as the bread and butter of a corporation while identifying and meeting changing consumer needs.

If there is a market for a modified product, you can readily go through the relevant sections of the business plan outline in step one and analyse whether your core business would be affected by this product or service variation, and if so, for better or for worse. Then make your decision accordingly.

Here is a sample Commonality Survey to help you think about your current clients in terms of what clues they can give you for choosing new clients. The survey can be adapted for past/lost clients.

Present/existing client Commonality Survey

Date. ....

Name of client. .... Distance from your office. ....

National, yes/no. Multinational, yes/no.

Subsidiary of. ....

Names of people you relate to and what it is that you like and dislike about each of them.

Name. .... Like. ....

Dislike. ....

Name. .... Like. ....

Dislike. ....

Name. .... Like. ....

Dislike. ....

What does the client think of your company's performance and relationships with their people? ....

Their industry sector. ....

Their product or service. ....

Size of company by revenue. ....

Ranking in Top 100. ..... Top 200. ..... Top 500. .....

Ranking up/down from previous years (explain). ....

Staff numbers now. .... Growing/declining? ....

Expenditure now with your company. ....

Growing or declining in expenditure? ....

Client is/is not profitable (explain). ....

....

How do you see the next 2, 3, 5 years with this client?

Will they grow with you, fade away, remain about the same? (explain) ....

....

....

Explain why/how the client should be.

Kept. ....

Replaced. ....

Revitalised. ....

If you owned the client company, what changes would you make? ....

....

....

Use what you have seen in these analyses to find more of the clients you want.

Market research

> *'Let others praise ancient times; I am glad I was born in these."* Ovid (43 B.C.–A.D. 18)

You might wish to initiate market research about a particular product or about your company's standing with consumers as measured against similar companies. Market research can provide clues to the future. Following are some of the questions you might wish to ask in focus groups with your own customers and those of similar companies.

Focus groups are used to find out what customers like and dislike and why they buy this product instead of that, as well as other issues such as quality of customer/client service, staff attitudes, product knowledge.

The groups usually meet for two hours and provide considerable insight for future action such as extended market research surveys.

> *"Get your facts first, then you can distort them as you please."* Mark Twain (1835–1910)

Questions could include

What type of organisations are producing similar products/services to yours?

What are their clients' expectations and perceptions of these?

Are there regional purchasing variations? If so, what are they? And what causes them?

What do your clients think of you as opposed to your competition?

What do your clients see themselves needing in the future?

Would your clients buy again? If not, why? If yes, why? And over what period of time?

And most of all, why are people not buying from you when you have a product or service that would suit them well?

The answers to these and other questions will allow you to move your business forward from a position of knowledge. You can use the findings to help you decide many issues, among them:

- Your overall business plan and marketing strategy.
- The products and services that should be continued, discontinued, developed or enhanced.
- Likely areas for new-client development, taking local variations into account. For instance in the colder part of large countries, people readily go on winter holidays, because they already have warm clothes in their wardrobe.

In the warmer zones they prefer to go on tropical island cruises, because they live in a sun-filled, warm climate and dress accordingly. If you were providing travel, you would promote different holidays in different regions, thereby getting more value for your advertising and promotional dollar.

- The selling cycle. Is it the same all year, or seasonal?
- The required research, advertising, sales promotion, events, database/direct marketing, telemarketing, training, merchandising activities and the staff or outside consultancies needed to make it all happen.
- The public relations, corporate communication positioning activities and the staff/consultancies needed.

The results of your market research will likely increase the quality of your business and marketing plans, their implementation and thereby the flow of qualified leads to salespeople. This research will also ultimately provide customers with products and services they require.

Consider doing research on a daily basis to keep you up to date with what clients, customers (and prospects) are experiencing so that rapid action can stop any problems before they set in.

This daily research can be captured by printing a number of cards with your vision statement on them and the simple question, "Did your visit match our vision?" Ask also for their name and phone number and ring those who answered, both yes and no. It is good to get the good news to prepare you for the bad!

Make research work for you every day

> *"Either I've been missing something or nothing has been going on."* Karen Elizabeth Gordon

Plan to have ongoing market research every day. If you are a retailer it can be very simple. Design an easy-to-answer, short questionnaire that your customers can fill in at reception or while they are waiting for their credit card to be approved or for their purchases to be added up and bagged. Or they might take it home to respond to later or be surveyed in the car park as they leave.

I recently developed a research questionnaire for a major retailer. When asked, "Was this store comfortable to be in—not too hot or too cold?" two of the shoppers complained that the stores were cold. Later the management agreed that they themselves had visited their stores to buy personal items in winter and had found the staff "all rugged up against the cold".

Now the staff and the customers can look forward to being warm next winter, just from two responses to such a simple (but very important) question. Similarly, I was shopping in Bloomingdales in New York, and the boutique area was so hot I felt sick. As I gave up and left, I commented to the attendant. She said she had been complaining about it for years, but no-one would do anything. Her sales were dreadful in the winter because of the heat and not much better in the summer because of the air-conditioning.

If you are in the professional services industry, send out with your clients' accounts a survey checking for satisfaction. I once used a direct marketing consultancy whose accounting system changed suddenly to billing us progressively throughout the time of the project.

The company was so slow in doing the work that the progressive billing was entirely irrelevant—I had not yet seen anything tangible! And since there was no cut-off period, it was hard to figure out what we had paid for and what was still coming in.

If the company concerned had put in a survey form asking if clients were having any trouble with the changeover, the troubles would have eased. They might also have asked if we were satisfied with the work done. I would have told them yes, but that it was done far too slowly. As it was, I just got better and faster at doing more of the projects myself.

Key points to remember

Choose your prospects wisely through the Commonality Survey. Find out why your competitors' clients are not currently buying from you. All your prospects in your contact system must be there for very good reasons. Constantly research your clients, customers and prospects for their needs, and meet those needs before your competitors do.

For many years people asked the same question about contacting prospects, "How often should I be in touch?" For many years people answered, "As often as is necessary", which was no help. The next chapter solves that mystery once and for all. Read on for what is the key to the whole process of new-business contacting—the regular, relentless follow-up within a three-month period.

Step Four

Stay in contact regularly and relentlessly within ninety days

> *"Work is so much more fun than fun."*
> Noel Coward (1899–1973)

The equivalent barge-along-the-canal prospect management system with a wide band of prospects will work no matter what your business. Start by researching who is most likely to want your product (as in the Commonality Survey). Then keep in touch regularly and relentlessly within ninety days—more often if you wish, but never let ninety days go by without contact—which is approximately sixty working days. Proven by Saatchi's over twenty-five years and by me during my time with the Inter-Continental Hotel Group, this ninety-day timing is the missing link in most people's contact management process. It was certainly missing in mine for far too many years.

What Saatchi & Saatchi found over that long period of following up on their chosen corporations, was that the people within had a clear enough memory of the previous call and conversation for up to 90 days. After that it was as though the mind had cleared itself of all memory.

L J Hooker's general manager in Sydney had a similar experience. He and I had met, then our next appointment was moved and rebooked for the first week of the fourth month following. The first thing he said was that he was going to put the whole of L J Hooker on the 90 day cycle. When I queried why, he said that for 90 days I had been clear in his mind—almost as though I were in the room with him when he thought of me, but on the first day of the fourth month, I had shrunk to the size of a jelly bean!

In Hong Kong we stayed in touch with 100,000 mothers every

three months, advising them that their babies were growing slowly and steadily and it was time to move up to the next size of disposable diaper. We enclosed a "price-off" voucher to make the next purchase very affordable.

Through this quarterly educational program, we grew our market share from 13% to 42% and each point was worth US$1million over the life cycle of the product.

When I was working in Melbourne, representing the Inter-Continental Hotel Group worldwide (some 60 hotels), I called on the major players in the travel industry every day. Through reward, recognition and an almost perfect reservations system, we grew the business from 200 room nights per month to 2001.

Then New York head office wanted the training program on how we did it, so I was locked away for several months writing, designing, refining and getting ready. For three months those room nights stayed at their highest point and then in the first week of the fourth month the bookings crashed.

The travel industry gave all the business—and more—to the Hilton Hotel group who came through at that time with a special promotion. The Hilton Group must have been amazed at the results.

When I met David Miln at Saatchi & Saatchi in London and he said that they had found the ninety-day cycle was the maximum time for staying in touch, I said, "I have that graph", and told him the whole wonderful and sad story of the Inter-Continental Hotel bookings.

We shook hands on the truth of the ninety-day cycle and agreed that when people have developed trust and belief in you and your product, and then you walk away, you can lose all that you have gained and more.

In London at Saatchi's executive recruitment company I used the 90 day cycle for having open days and top-name speakers like Charles Handy and Sir John Harvey Jones, to attract prospects into the offices of MSL, where they would meet and get to know the staff. With 400 major companies as our prospects, we gained ten of them within two years.

In New York, where my client had been "choking the life out of too few friends", we identified 8000 more prospects through the Commonality Survey across America and contacted them by mail and follow-up phone call every three months. By the 5th cycle of mailing and phone calls, we were getting around 60% acceptance to appointments.

Make your new-business program an integral part of your daily operations and you can choose clients you want to work with as the opportunities arrive from your regular, relentless, creative and caring contact process, spread over sixty working days (or less if you wish).

Even if your customers and prospects will probably not buy again for a few years (for example, another car), you still have to keep in touch once every three months so that you'll be in the running when they are ready to purchase again. In South Africa a client commented that he had been buying new BMWs for seven years and had never had a contact of any sort from the seven agents he had used in that time. Note that both clients and prospects must be contacted within the three-month period.

Leave your clients in your prospecting system. Do not shift them into a separate "done-and-forgotten" file. Remember that they are somebody else's prospects. Remember too that you get more business from people who are already buying from you—so your clients are still prospects in that sense also.

Make this Saatchi & Saatchi barge-down-the-canal system work for you

> *"There are very few people who don't become more interesting when they stop talking."* Mary Lowry

Build a broad band of prospects. Consider now how many people you have been contacting as prospects. Have you been pursuing a few, instead of building a series of friendships with many? Or have you already got around one hundred and fifty to two hundred well-chosen prospects? Use the Commonality Survey (Step 3) to ensure you are talking to the right people.

Three is the magic number. Have you been contacting your prospects within three months or less, or only when you have time? Have they learned to trust you because you always stay in contact, regularly and in a professional manner? Or are you an infrequent caller because you are too busy?

No more will your new business be stop/start/give up 'til next time. You simply take your wide band of prospects (say, one hundred and eighty) and divide by the number of working days in three months: being sixty. Quite suddenly you only have to make three or four contacts a day to have a regular, relentless, successful new-business program.

If you chose a forty-day span you make around five attempts each day. Of course, no-one is ever there when you phone, so send a card, a letter, a relevant PR piece or your brochure and a note saying that you will be in touch again within three (or two or one) months. Be sure to enclose your business card every time. Think—how many have you lost/mislaid in the last few years?

The hunter/farmer relationship to new-business development

In the early stages of starting a business, entrepreneurs both hunt down the prospects and then handle (farm) them as clients. If you are doing both, you will most likely find you have a natural preference for one or the other.

When your business has grown to the point that you have too much to handle, you can replace yourself with someone more suited to the role you like least. If you prefer hunting, keep the hunting/prospecting role for yourself. If you'd rather be back at the ranch mending fences, caring for the livestock, harvesting grain, checking the finances, supervising the staff, then stay in that farming role.

If the wrong person gets into either role, the hunting will be ineffective and prospects who do become clients will be left unattended. There is an easy way to define who would fit the hunting role. Successful hunters are people who genuinely believe that the prospect's needs can be met by their organisation alone. They are always looking ahead to their next challenge, ready to make an extra detour for excitement.

On the other hand, farmers are there to nurture clients and to reinforce the idea that customers have made the right decision in choosing their company. What's more, farmers are content to play this steady, ongoing nurturing role over a long period of time.

More questions to help you decide whether you are a hunter or a farmer

Are you a hunter?
Are you excited and thrilled by the chase?
Is winning everything?

Is each day an adventure?
Do you live on the edge and love it?
Do you enjoy being by yourself?
Do you have so many things to do that you barely have time to sleep?
If so, in all probability, you're a hunter.

> *"I hate the outdoors. To me the outdoors is where the car is."*
> Will Durst

Are you a farmer?
Do you prefer to build relationships rather than say "hi" and run?
Are you more comfortable in known surroundings than coping with new countries, new languages, new foods?
Do you prefer an organised day to always having to rush to another appointment?
Are you quite shy of new people and prefer to be with those you know?
If all this is true of you, it seems likely you will flourish in the farming role.

Hunters and farmers are compatible because they both desire the success of the business, but different in their need for excitement.

Key points to remember

- Build relationships regularly and relentlessly, creatively and caringly. Make regular contact within ninety days. You can wait less than ninety days if you wish, but never more than ninety days, otherwise you lose more than you gain.
- Divide your total prospects by the sixty working days in three months and see, hear and feel how easily you can incorporate one hundred and fifty to two hundred prospects into your daily business life. Three or four attempted contacts a day, and it is done.
- Keep moving—simply send a note, card, whatever, if you do not reach your prospects by phone, and keep on regularly and relentlessly. One day you will get through to those well-chosen

likely buyers and they will remember you from your regular communications. Always enclose your business card.

Recently I was talking to the owner of a company who had taken responsibility for their corporate brochure. Three years had gone by and still there was no first draft. He felt that he just could not get going—he didn't seem to have a beginning. Without a beginning you can't have a middle or an end, so he was stuck.

"To start the process, what about your single-minded proposition?" I asked. "Quite simply, what does your company do for your clients?"

Good question, so we got on with the process of finding out. The next chapter will help you do the same.

Step Five

The "single-minded" proposition

> *"It's not true that life is one damn thing after another—it is one damn thing over and over."*
>
> Edna St Vincent Millay (1892–1950)

What quite simply does your company do from your client/customer's point of view? Once you know, you can tell the rest of the world, clearly, loudly and often.

A major benefit of hearing from your clients and customers constantly is that these people will help you find the best way to describe your product or service by how they talk about it. Your need for that key phrase becomes evident when you are designing your communications and public relations program.

That key phrase is called either the "single-minded proposition" or the "unique selling point". At Saatchi & Saatchi in Hong Kong we used to call it (but not in front of the bosses) "simple-minded" proposition, because it stated so simply what the product or service does for the buyer.

Note that I said for the buyer, not for the company selling the product or service. When you have the key phrase down, it will lead you into a corporate statement for all your promotional activities.

If you are having trouble with thinking about the benefits from the point of view of the person paying the bill, think of red roses. The single-minded reason for sending **red** roses (or so I am told in workshops) is sex and guilt. I see no reason to disagree! Yet most florists promote their wares generally and their delivery service primarily.

One memorable day, I did a workshop on the single-minded

proposition with an advertising agency. My brief to them was to create the name and the tag line (from the single-minded proposition) for a business that sold **only** red roses—24 hours a day, seven days a week, 365 days a year. Plus the balloons and cards that went with such a purchase.

Their response? The name was to be "Bad Boys" and the tag line—from understanding that red roses were about sex and guilt—was to be, "We get you into and out of trouble, 24 hours a day."

See how easy it is to define a tag line when you know why people part with hard-earned money for your product or service? And miraculously, when you are looking for a further example, you see it in the most amazing places. On a motorway, there it was, a huge poster:

Minolta—we understand the office. Printers, faxes, photocopiers.

Ever after I have asked my clients, "What is it that you understand from the buyer's point of view?" and quote the Minolta example. In only a matter of minutes, you too can achieve a similar powerful tag line. In fact, when I am consulting with companies, I ask them to do it just before lunch and it takes a very few minutes! Such a difference from the days and weeks that we used to spend thinking, talking, arguing at Saatchi and Saatchi Advertising before we got even close.

Stop now and ask yourself what it is that you understand. If you are in real estate you could say, "We understand London W1 housing", or "We understand New York office space". If you are a beautician you could say, "We understand your need to be beautiful". If you're a lawyer you could say, "We understand your need for a fair solution".

Without this thinking about what it is you understand from the buyer's point of view, you get an internal think-tank kind of single-minded proposition.

So spend time, really spend time, listening for the key phrase which will provide the jumping-off point for that simple-minded statement of what it is you provide to your clients or customers.

Ring your clients, ask them what it is that you understand from **their** point of view.

Then when you create any literature, any leaflet, any brochure, any annual report, any item that is bought by the public, be sure to include that simple-minded statement.

Put it in there, boldly and frequently. It tells buyers exactly why they should buy from you—and they will understand your statement because of its simplicity and repetition.

Now look around you for advertising which shows a clear sense of purpose ... one which could have come from a "single-minded proposition". Look around for advertising where the product is presented in the buyers' terms, unfailingly and without deviation. You may not find too many examples, but when you do, they are powerful.

And work at incorporating your company name into a tag line—the one that you will create on hearing from the buying public what it is they think you provide.

For example, if you have a disposable diaper as your product and the parents say that it keeps their baby free of nappy rash, a linked statement in one typeface like, "Comfie—the dry one", would help the consumer remember you better than, say, "The dry one". The latter statement could be for a beer, a wine, or a clothes dryer.

When you watch ads on TV see if you can decide what the product is with the sound turned off. If you can, it is a great advertisement; if you can't, it should not be on air.

> *"Victory goes to the player who makes the next-to-last mistake."* Savielly Grigorievitch Tartakover, 1887–1956

Make the single-minded proposition work for you

Write out three quite simple statements that you think express what your company does, from the point of view of the buyer. Imagine that you have paid for a huge highway sign at the cost of a million dollars a day. Passing motorists have one second to see your message and come and buy because of it. Now write to make that million dollars work for you:

1. ....

2. ....

3. ....

Now ring three great clients and ask them what they, quite simply, get from your company. Write in their ideas, statements, comments, whatever.

1. ....

....

2. ....

....

3. ....

....

Example: An advertising agency client discussed what their clients would say about them and decided that it would be "Argumentative, difficult, stubborn".

When they got up the courage to ask their clients they heard, "The best, committed to excellence, extraordinary attention to the problem, exceptional solutions, great profits".

Is there any similarity between what your clients say and what you wrote? Would their statements be better on your million-dollar poster? Would your clients' comments help you state your speciality so well that many more dollars would flow into your organisation as a result?

If so, use what you have heard to create your all-powerful tag line statement. Then test that tag line with other clients and prospects. If it "hits the spot" you now have that simple phrase with which to describe why people should buy from you. Use it verbally and in all your corporate literature.

Acknowledge the clients and prospects who helped you. Write a letter of thanks, send a gift. Now why not set up a Board of Advisers? You could ask these top clients and helpful prospects to be part of your Advisory Board. Meet once a month for dinner at your expense and have your Board advise you from their point of view.

Include your bank manager, likely prospects and other non-relevant business people whom you respect for their business experience and knowledge, as well as their straight talk. Your gift to them for donating their time may be $50–$100 each time you meet, on top of the dinner. That makes everyone take you and their responsibilities as advisers seriously.

West Coast Coolers provide an example of how an outside person can see things differently. I hear they were developed in this way: wine growers in California had an excess of wine and asked Faith Popcorn in New York to help them come up with new products. In a wide-ranging think-tank group, a hairdresser mused, "Why not add fruit juice to wine, the way we add orange juice to champagne?" The rest is multi-million dollar history.

Key points to remember

Really work at finding that critical "single-minded proposition". It is a three-step process. First ask your current clients or customers what it is that they get from you. Then when you hear a common theme, you create from it a tag line that is directly linked (in the same typeface) with your company name.

Test that tag line with clients and non-clients. If it makes sense to them, you then use it in all types of written communication. Now form a loosely chosen Board of Advisers and enjoy their company and their advice.

"Use your single-minded proposition in all types of written communication" brings us to the next chapter which is: "Look like the company you want to be."

Step Six

Look like the company you want to be

> *"In six pages I can't even say hello."* James Michener

Near where I lived in New York on 57th Street, there were two restaurants quite close together. Both had beautiful floral arrangements in the window. One window was well lit, the other in semi-darkness. The first restaurant was full of people, the second usually half empty.

Getting your corporate look right can be as simple as the effect of a light bulb. When you choose your potential clients and customers well and design your materials accordingly, that impression will make the difference in convincing them to buy from you.

Desks worldwide look about the same: covered with white sheets of paper printed with black ink. It's a lot easier to attract attention if your promotional pieces are bigger, more colourful, and more professional-looking than the many other communications on your prospect's desk. The fact is that with the right colours, design, copy and layout you can take a company that was registered today and make it look as stable and as solid as a Rolls-Royce.

Similarly, you can reposition an older company to look jazzy, exciting and new with different colours, design, copy and layout if the product has changed sufficiently to warrant it.

It is all what the eye sees in a split second and the brain believes. Now you **can** take control of your corporate look.

The contents of your letter

> *"Writing is easy. All you do is stare at a blank sheet of paper until drops of blood form on your head."* Gene Fowler (1890–1960)

A good letter has a beginning, a middle and an end. First, tell recipients why you want them to read the letter. Next, tell them what you want them to know. Close by telling them what action will come next: that you will call them for an appointment; that they should fill in an enclosed form if they would like to buy your product; that they should call or reply by a certain date, etc.

Assume the recipients of your letter are busy and tired. Don't write a letter that leaves them wondering why you wrote or what they should do to get what you're offering. Make it easy for people to continue the relationship with you.

Don't use flowery language. The message in the words, "He was delayed by the breakdown of his motor vehicle" is more easily conveyed to busy people as, "His car broke down, so he was late." People respect easy, clear communications.

If you want readers to continue onto a second or third page, make sure to end the page in mid-sentence, so the reader has to turn over to complete the message. This is an old Reader's Digest technique and it works.

The appearance of your letter

> *"He writes so well he makes me feel like putting my quill back in my goose."* Fred Allen 1894–1956

How do you get your letter read? Easy—keep it simple and short. Think of any printed communication as having three elements: a coastline (the shape of the words), land mass (the size of the paragraphs), sky and ocean (the white spaces surrounding the paragraphs). We read words by the shape of their letters, by their coastline.

In a word like "pretty" there is an interesting coastline between the p, the ts and the y, which makes it an easily recognisable word. Now try to read this: PRETTY. See how much more difficult it is to read all in capitals? That is because we now have to read each letter separately, instead of speeding across a known shape. Our reading is slowed down considerably as a result.

Underlining, too, makes words almost completely illegible.

When you want someone to take notice of what you have written, put the words you want to stand out **in bold, heavy type**.

The human eye (and mind) likes peace. It likes lots of white space. It is no accident that most stationery is restful white or cream-coloured. Leave big margins left and right. Have paragraphs of no more than sixty words. That's six lines of ten words.

Write short sentences and simple words. Use a typeface that has serifs, which are short, curved or straight cross-lines at the top and bottom of most of its letters. Serifs help us decipher the letters; that's why newspapers, magazines and this book use type-faces with serifs.

People read most easily the way they read most commonly. Since the preferred reading for pleasure is usually newspapers and magazines and we are therefore used to the serif typefaces used in these publications, make sure you use a serif typeface when you go to print. It can be useful, too, to publish reports and copies of speeches in double columns, as in magazines.

For instance, I have on my desk two publications of recent speeches. One is laid out across the page with small margins, in very elongated, and single-spaced, skinny paragraphs of two to three lines.

The other is in two central columns per page, with interesting quotes from the speech as "take-outs" in the wide margins. The second one is so much more readable than the first. The first I didn't even finish—I tried, I just couldn't make sense of it.

When a glance at your printed page shows lots of sky and ocean and little land mass, you have a communication that people will want to read. The same usually applies to advertising. Use lots of white space, a few precise words and images and you're a winner.

Make good-looking letters happen in your organisation

> *"I don't want any yes-men around me. I want everybody to tell me the truth even if it costs them their jobs."*
> Sam Goldwyn, 1882–1974

Check the appearance and content of your letters. Go to your filing basket or cabinet and pull out at random a handful of recent letters sent to clients, prospects, suppliers, debtors, creditors, whomever. Imagine receiving these letters yourself and ask these questions:

Are the letters excellent communications at first glance by virtue of quality paper, typeface and printing? Does your company name, logo and address stand out clearly? Can people easily find your phone and fax numbers?

I had a client in America whose letterhead and invoices were so muddled that they received letters and cheques made out to their prominently stated street address; their company name was lost among their overseas affiliates. Are the letters well laid out, with small paragraphs, big margins, good space between the paragraphs? Does the letter look peaceful and welcoming at first glance?

Are all the sentences clear in their intent and content? Are the spelling and grammar correct? Are simple words used throughout? Does the reader know why you have written and what is to be done next? Is the tone pleasant and helpful? Did you make a friend in every case by sending these letters?

Now you may wish to look at your incoming mail and see how many meet these basic standards. Perhaps you will see some really good examples of great-looking and great-sounding letters from your associates; then again you may realise that you are well ahead of the average.

Colour in corporate communications

> *"I don't know the key to success, but the key to failure is trying to please everybody."* Bill Cosby

All colours have their place, but their effects on us are so immediate that if you use them wrongly you can destroy the image you're trying to project. If you want to look solid, stable, powerful, royal blue seems to fit the image.

If instead you want to make the recipient feel gentled and cared for by your company's communication, bright red would be too strong. Soft burgundy and gold could be just right.

In my design work I have found that using red and blue together sends out a message of solid, stable and secure, plus a hint of danger and excitement.

For you to think about your corporate design, here are some general tips about using colour, gleaned from my years of experience in designing communications for clients:

Pale blue and **pale pink** are reminiscent of childhood and are often used effectively in catalogues of children's clothing. In Sydney I have seen pink concrete mixing trucks and it is always hard to think of that concrete making solid, stable, secure buildings.

For the many people who love music, the Russian painter Kandinsky said that light blue is like the sound of a flute.

Yellow means sunlight, warmth, a lovely day. However, most of us do not see sunlight as yellow, but as enhancing the colours around us. Bright yellow is not a colour many people want to live with; it seems brash in its strongest shades. Thus, yellow (or gold) is better as an accessory to another, more attractive colour; you might use gold leaf on royal blue, burgundy or green.

Royal blue as we have said, tends to represent solidity and power, stability and security. It is cool and calm and very good to look at. Use it if you are a solid, stable, secure organisation (or wish to look like one).

Kandinsky likened the deepening shades of blue to the cello, a double bass and darkest of all, an organ.

Green is a colour that surrounds us wherever we go: green trees, green grass, green leaves. Green is peaceful but calls out to be highlighted by an array of vibrant flower colours—red, pink, apricot, yellow or gold. If you plan to use green in corporate materials, use other warmer colours with it; otherwise, your communications may seem dull and passive at a second glance.

Imagine, for instance, being in a jungle with no tumbling flowers, no highly coloured birds. At first it would be restful, then quite boring.

Brown is earth-coloured, warm, solid, and sensible, but most people do not find it impressive. Avoid using brown to express a corporate identity, unless it is for a caring environmental product, such as a paper bag. For example, the Body Shop gives brown paper bags to their customers.

Red in its blue-red or orange-red tonings is a colour some people love; to others it suggests fire, danger, warlike behaviour and "don't touch"!

In business, people want to know that their needs will be met, that whatever is troubling them will be remedied by your company or your product. Red, when it predominates, can give the opposite message. However, used in moderation or softened to burgundy or maroon, it can be warm and firm at the same time.

Light red, says Kandinsky, compares with trumpets, strong and ringing; pure red with the singing notes of a violin; and orange-red with the angelus or the notes of an old violin.

Consider how people fall asleep (almost) at green lights, but have the urge to charge through red ones. (Perhaps stop lights should be green and go lights red!)

Violet, mauve, purple, grey and **grey-greens** are considered by many people to signal mourning, depending on the intensity of the colours. In our Russian friend's belief, violet is an English horn or the deep notes of wood instruments, such as the bassoon.

Where a lot of white is added to the above colours, and the effect is silver grey or pale mauve or soft green-grey, the feeling is more of an early morning light. These quite gentle colours can be ideal for expressing soft, emotional products.

Look at the design and the colours of the materials you receive from other companies. Sort them into two categories: pieces that impress you as having come from a quality enterprise, and those that don't.

Notice what factors influence you to decide that a particular communication comes from a business which knows how to get its message across effectively.

A recap on the subliminal messages of colour:

Royal blue: Calm, stable, serene, cool, peaceful, trustworthy, restful, honourable.

Deep red: Warlike, dangerous, hot, passionate, exciting, aggressive, vibrant, prohibitive, stimulating.

Bright orange: Warm, sensual, joyful, passionate, lively, full of energy, welcoming.

Yellow: Sunny, cheerful, bright but with an undertone of cowardice and deceit.

Green: Restful, cool, calm, balanced, fresh, but boring after a while and also tinged with jealousy.

Indigo/violet/purple: Royal, dignified, mysterious, powerful, wise, solitary, with strong overtones of control, authority and grief.

Grey/mauve/grey-green: Sad, old, mournful, withdrawn, lonely, dull, without life or passion.

Silver grey/pale mauve/light green-grey: Diffusive, gentle, touching, soft.

Black: Powerful, sophisticated, dramatic, withdrawn, serious, dignified, elegant; yet also sad, evil, wicked and gloomy.

White: Pure, innocent, youthful, faithful, simple, honest, peaceful.

Brown: Dirty, dull, boring, unexciting, worthy, uncompromising.

The three primary colours

> *"Give me a museum and I will fill it."* Pablo Picasso

The three primaries are the boldest, strongest colours. If you ever have trouble remembering what the three primary colours are (the colours from which all other colours grow), simply remember "ryb" pronounced "rib". These stand for red, yellow and blue.

Now look into the colours of the rainbow and meet Roy G. Biv = **R**ed, **o**range, **y**ellow, **g**reen, **b**lue, **i**ndigo, **v**iolet.

To remember the other colours that the primary colours of red, yellow and blue make together is simple: the colour in the middle is created by the two primary colours on either side.

Orange sits between red and yellow; green sits between yellow and blue; and indigo/violet would sit between blue and red if the rainbow were joined as a circle.

Using this "seated between" imagery, you can recall that red and yellow get together to make orange; yellow and blue mix in to make green; then blue hops around the corner to meet red and out pops indigo or violet, depending on the mix.

You may well ask, why does this matter?

It is all to do with creating the point of greatest contrast: you use colours that stand out against the background to draw the eye of the reader to your single-minded statement or powerful graphic design, be it on a brochure, flyer, advertisement, or point of sale.

The primary colours, red, yellow and blue, and the secondary colour of orange (mixed from red and yellow) are the most intense and make a good background for your contrasting colours.

Primary colours as background

Let's imagine royal blue as your brochure background colour; white stands out against it more dramatically than any other colour. Now take red as a background; again white stands out against it vividly. Take yellow or orange as a background colour; black stands out well, better than white would.

Primary colours as foreground

If we reverse all this and have a background of white, we find that blue, red and black stand out well. On a background of black, yellow, orange and white stand out well. We can see that black on dark blue disappears, yellow on red does not work well (these colours seem to "eat" each other up) and red and black together looks dull.

While I agree that black and white are not primary colours, black is the absorber of all the colours and as such is the perfect contrast for white—which is the reflector of all colours. Black is seen as the colour of darkness because it represents the end of all colours. White is seen as the colour of light, the morning awakening, because it takes nothing in and gives everything back.

For this real physical reason, black is a much hotter experience as a fabric than white. Black takes in the heat (light rays) of the sun, white reflects the heat back. A black fabric worn in the tropics is unbearable; white fabric is much cooler to wear.

A shining black car is seen as powerful and deadly, a shining white car as pure and clean. (Consider a black funeral car v. a white wedding car.) A shiny or dull black brochure gives a lethal message. A shiny or even flat white brochure expresses purity instantly. These two "colours" give out more immediate and clearer messages than any other colour.

Secondary colours for your corporate image

Let's recap on the secondary colours: orange, green, indigo/violet. Could we use these as background or foreground colours? Yes indeed, if they represent the imagery we want to express.

An orange brochure would look good with contrasted colours such as black, blue, green or white. A green brochure could look great with flower colours incorporated, such as apricot, orange, gold, red. And indigo/violet is so close to blue that red, orange and yellow would be good contrasts. The field is open to whatever you want to use, providing you are satisfied that the image sent out represents your company.

You will notice that the contrasting colours which work well are the ones with the opposite degree of warmth. The warm colours of red, orange and yellow contrast well with the cool colours of green, blue, indigo and violet. No need to struggle with what goes with what. Just choose two that look good together in terms of intense contrast and they will automatically be the cool and the warm.

As for white and black, the cool shades of green and the three blues (royal, indigo and violet) go well with white providing they are enhanced by touches of warm colours; the warm shades of yellow, orange and red go well with black.

The reverse does not work so well when you try to put cool with cool, warm with warm. Green with black or blue with black cannot create enough contrast to immediately attract the eye.

Similarly yellow with white is too close to create a powerful contrast. Orange, which is made with the two warm colours, red and yellow, and has an incredible strength of its own, works brilliantly with black and very well with white. Green, on the other hand, is made with one warm and one cool colour (yellow and blue) so it does not have that intensity of effect on the eye and the mind and needs a lot of support from other warmer colours to remain attractive to the viewer.

With any colour, if you want to pale its intensity, simply add white. Red loses its strength to become pink, orange mutes to apricot, yellow weakens to cream, green becomes insipid, blue is washed out, indigo and violet are muted to remind one of dark shadows, and black becomes grey. Mix up the three primaries (red, yellow and blue) and you will get brown.

Understanding the power of colour

Imagine the flags of various countries paled down with white. The American flag would lose all its glory as would the British Union Jack. The Japanese Rising Sun, bright red, would fade to a pale pink sunset. The French Tricolour of strong blue, white and red would fade to baby blue and baby pink. No power left in any of these!

This weakening of colours in your mind's eye is designed to show you how strongly the right colours and design attract, how powerfully the wrong colours repel.

From this experience you will readily see and feel how well a company can be served by choosing relevant colours and design for its corporate material.

And the reverse—how badly a company can be served by incongruent colours and design.

Getting your main message across

To recap: to draw attention to your message, put it at the point of greatest contrast in the space that is seen first, such as the front cover of a brochure.

Always contrast lightest with darkest if you want to draw attention to your product or service with a picture or with printed words.

The eye will obey your command. If the basic colour of your brochure is royal blue and you use a large block of big, white type against it, the eye will go immediately to that point of greatest contrast. The eye obeys, it simply cannot help itself.

In this instance, if you have a secondary message, make its white print slightly smaller than the first main bold white message and the eye will go there next. However, if you use dark blue with black print, that will be the last thing the eye will see.

White waves against a dark blue sky; a rich red rock against a pale blue sky—these stand out vividly. Imagine handkerchiefs of light and dark shades in a dark suit pocket and see for yourself how strongly the light handkerchief draws your eye.

Use your single-minded proposition on all your printed material.

When you have your single-minded proposition, use this

design technique to make that message stand out on your brochure or flyer.

For example, International Courier Brokers decided that their single-minded proposition was, "We understand your courier needs, nationally and internationally". When we designed their new corporate ID we made good use of that statement on their letterhead, business cards and envelopes, plus their invoices and statements and presentation folders, using red and blue on white as their colours.

Solid and stable or bright and jazzy?

It is so important to get your image right at first glance. Decide whether you want to be solid and long-lasting, or bright, jazzy and new. When you have made that decision, here is how you effectively present your new image:

The location of your wording and graphics is important. Place them on the right side of the front cover of your corporate brochure and you're seen as powerful and long-lasting.

Put the same wording or graphics on the left side and you're seen as young, snappy and fresh. The reason for this is that what is seen on the right-hand side of the page is acknowledged by the left-hand, analytical side of the brain.

Similarly, what is seen on the left-hand side of the page goes through to the right-hand, creative side of the brain. Colours have a similar impact: jazzy fluorescent colours give a completely different impression than solid, sensible colours.

Try this for example. Imagine looking at a painting which has a large jagged rock on the right-hand side, a lake in the middle and a coconut palm on the left.

Now swap the rock and the tree over. The tree is on the right, the rock on the left of the lake. For me the harmony and power of the first painting is lost in the second. The tree looks too thin and frail for the "power" position, the rock too big and solid for the "creative" position. How does it look to you?

Test your designs on clients and prospects. Ask them for their first-glance impressions. Do not ask your colleagues or friends—they're not objective enough because they're too close to the subject.

Ask "what is it?" questions. What is it about the brochure you like? What is it that you do not like? What is it about our product that you like? What is it that we could improve? The value of the "what is it?" question is that it is a non-defensive enquiry.

We are genuinely interested in hearing their answers. If the response is negative at any time, do not defend yourself; simply keep asking "what is it?" questions.

You can transfer this "what is it?" technique to other personal and business aspects of your life. It is an excellent negotiating technique, because you get real answers. You no longer have to second-guess the issues.

For instance, if your client, customer or prospect says, "I don't like your price", simply ask, "What is it about the price that you don't like?"

Instead of defending your price, you are listening for their response. If they say it is too high, ask them, "By how much is it too high?" or "Compared to what is it too high?" In probing and feeding back their own words, you have lost the desire to argue and are actively and positively responding to the customer's needs.

Assess your responses to the mail you receive, in terms of colour and copy. Why do some pieces strike a positive note, while others cry out to be scrapped immediately? What does written material that is brassy and cheap say about a company? What about cool, serene-looking material?

By placing copy in the proper position and using the best colours for your purpose, you can ensure the harmony of your communications.

Use the best quality paper you can possibly afford for your corporate communications. Everything that looks cheap says "cheap" about you. Everything you do well is to your credit ever after.

A business associate for whom I designed her corporate ID phoned me recently to say that she had won a major piece of business. Her client said that they remembered the energy of her letterhead and business card and decided she had the style and talent for the job. It can be that simple!

Brochures look best with a glossy finish, while smooth, matt paper is best for your letterhead. A company's written pieces reflect the personality and operating philosophy of the owners and managers, which is forcefully passed on to the reader, like it or not.

The Golden Line

About 2000 years ago, the Greek mathematician Pythagoras said that there was a natural law and order of design in life, and he called it "The Golden Mean". For the sake of design simplicity we will call it the Golden Line.

When you look at something beautiful, like a Vermeer painting, a Georgian house or a piece of jewellery in just the right spot on a coat, chances are that it is on the Golden Line.

Using the Golden Line is simple and it makes your printed material look terrific. It is based on thirds. This is how to do it:

Step one: Take a plain sheet of paper (the size of your normal letters) and fold it in half across the centre, **horizontally**.

Step two: Open the paper flat and fold the top edge down twice equally to the centre line, **horizontally**. This divides the top half of the paper into three equal sections above the centre.

Repeat from the bottom edge, so the paper is ultimately divided into six equal sections, three above the centre line and three below it. These are your **horizontal Golden Lines**.

Step 3: Open the paper flat again and fold it **vertically** in thirds. Thus, you will have divided the page into equal thirds from, say, right to left. Each of those thirds is a Golden Line on the **vertical**.

Your page will have folded oblong boxes made from the vertical and horizontal folds which you now can use as guidelines to lay out the key elements of your letterhead, brochure, flyer and anything else you have in mind.

Use the vertical left third of the sheet or the right third for your key messages—your company name and address and your single-minded statement about your product. Leave the centre blank—the eye likes white space, so create as much of it as you can.

Each of the Golden Line oblongs has mini-thirds within. So you can either work within your major Golden Line oblongs or you can go outside of the major lines to the mini lines. Similarly, you can fold the bottom third of the page into thirds again and use the middle third for your company address and details. Do not use the very bottom third, because faxes often lose that space.

You can use this technique to create a corporate image for yourself which, by the very pleasure of looking at it, expresses a harmony and style which says so much about you.

Fold your current letterhead as described above, and see whether your company name and address fits on or inside the Golden Line boxes you have created with your folded lines. If not, try shifting the detail until it looks harmonious to you, using the Golden Line boxes as guidelines.

Try not to use the centre for words or graphics when designing a brochure or flyer front cover. The brain cannot get a fix on information in the centre position. It needs to see things on the left or right side in order to decide whether you are bright, jazzy and new or solid, stable and secure.

A look of harmony is usually based on the thirds of the Golden Line, so leave the centre as a peaceful space in front cover design and see how often you can leave peaceful centre space inside your brochure also.

When using the vertical third lines to position your corporate statements, remember that on the right third, the message is seen as powerful, solid and stable. On the left third, jazzy, exciting and new.

The Golden Lines can guide you throughout any publication, any piece of literature that has to be designed.

Before I begin to write any copy, I lay out the vertical and the horizontal Golden Lines. Then I look at the brochure from a left-hand/right-hand side of the brain point of view. Are we to be seen as solid and well established or exciting and innovative?

If the first, I use the right-hand side of the page for the important points I want to make. If the latter, I move all the important words over to the left side. Power statements can look good on both sides—the choice of one or the other is a matter of the type of company you wish to portray.

For instance, I have a corporate brochure here with me as I write this. The company concerned is very solid, stable and international. They have listed all their international offices and addresses in small, small print down the left-hand side of the front cover of their brochure.

If they moved their international offices and addresses over to the right-hand side and stacked them top to bottom down the lower two thirds of the front cover, pointing to their single-minded proposition, the power of the piece would be far greater—especially done in larger print as well.

Currently it is thin and weak, and being on the left-hand side of the page, goes through to the right-hand creative side of the brain, sending out the message of weak and creative rather than big and strong and internationally stable.

Make your corporate literature stand out—look around for effective examples

> *"There is no pleasure in having nothing to do. The fun is having lots to do and not doing it."* John W. Raper

Getting the right look to your corporate materials will help you win appointments. Prospects will make snap judgments based on how your "window-dressing" looks to them. You will survive and prosper if their gut reaction is in your favour. Analyse your own gut reactions to material.

Go through all the possible places in your work area where old brochures and flyers might collect, on any product whatsoever. Pull them out and take them to a quiet place for your research.

Ring up every company you have ever thought of investing in through the share market and ask for their end-of-year financial report.

Clip coupons and send off for catalogues of every kind.

Go into car showrooms and take their brochures, especially the top-of-the-line cars.

Go into travel companies and take the brochures that make you want to leave town and the ones that make you want to stay home. Take the good, the bad and the ugly.

Collect, look, analyse, feel, read everything you can lay your hands on. Then compare your present corporate look with the way you would like it to be next time you print new material. You will find that you now have a naturally trained eye, that quality attracts and ugliness repels.

Once you have the fundamentals right, don't wait for perfection. Get on with making the best changes you can within the time and financial constraints you are under. Use the 80/20 rule. If it is eighty per cent okay, do it.

And check for the most likely smallest errors. For instance, when I was with Saatchi & Saatchi/MSL in London, we were passing out our business cards and noticed that nine out of nine had almost every bit of information in a different place on that small piece of white board. The MSL name and address was constant in spelling only.

So we liaised with the ordering department and sent the printing firm a sample of the one and only approved business card for all further orders. If any cards came back differently from then on, the bill was not paid. Problem solved.

Key points to remember

Decide whether your company should look solid, stable and secure or bright, jazzy and new. Then design on the Golden Line, choose relevant colours and position your copy with the left brain/right brain difference in mind to immediately give a congruent impression.

NEVER USE CAPITALS. They are difficult to read, and people won't read your message. Why is it difficult to read? Because CAPITALS/capitals take away the shape of a word as you can see above. No longer does the word have a coastline—it is just a block of copy.

When we are very young we read letter by letter—c a t—but as we get better at reading we read "cat" by the coastline of the word.

To get attention, **put it in bold instead. With no underlining because being bold is enough**. People read most easily in the way they read most commonly: books, magazines and newspapers use lower case except for some headings. Use wide margins, short paragraphs, simple words. Have a beginning, a middle and an end to all your communications.

For my own letterhead, and for two clients, I am now using only the right-hand two-thirds of the page, leaving the left-hand side empty and therefore available for a handwritten message, drawing attention to the key message in the copy. Then when I ring a prospect and ask if they received my letter, I remind them that it has a handwritten note in the margin. Instant recall!

"Sound like the company you want to be" is the next step in being congruent with your corporate look. You can't, for instance, create a Rolls-Royce image and have jazzy, casual staff on the phone and face to face without confusing the buyer.

Similarly if you have created a breezy, bright Ferrari look for yourself and you have slow, heavy staff, the buyer is going to react against that too.

Step Seven

Success in your calling cycles

> *"Nature has given us two ears but only one mouth."*
> Benjamin Disraeli (1804–1881)

Getting those appointments

Your primary method of contacting new business will be by phone. You will need to remember that these people are overwhelmed with responsibilities and awash with distracting and often irrelevant information.

Even if they like you and love what you can do for them, the pressures of daily life will keep them from focusing on giving you their business.

Not getting back in touch with you may have nothing to do with the value of your product or service and everything to do with the reality of all the other things competing for their attention.

Avoid falling in love with the names or reputations of particular companies; instead, fall in love with the number of companies you are going to contact. Achieve a high volume of prospects—a minimum of around two hundred per new-business person on staff—and keep in touch regularly and relentlessly.

Don't promise yourself that prospect number eighteen is the one you're going to win. That deflects your attention from the whole, just as dreaming of all the money you're going to make fogs up your mind when you're meant to be listening to a prospect's needs.

Determining who is the right person to talk to within an organisation may be the most difficult and time-consuming aspect of your new-business campaign. Making sure you're trying to reach the individual responsible for purchasing the goods or services you offer can be a long and tedious process, but it will save you time and money in the future.

The gatekeeper

"Gatekeepers" are the assistants or secretaries who screen calls and decide whether to put you through to the boss. They're a necessary part of the process. A lot of people think the gatekeeper is just someone you have to get around. The reality is that you're going to be coming into contact with gatekeepers over and over again. It's a mistake to treat these people lightly.

Gatekeepers talk with the boss; they are able to give the boss an impression of who you are. If you are pleasant, well prepared and patient, all of that will be conveyed to the boss. Gatekeepers can be wonderfully helpful or they can slow things up and keep you from getting to the main person.

The calling cycles

As we have stressed, a three-month call cycle must be established. Never go longer than three months without calling. Make sure that the conversation is friendly, courteous, polite and non-demanding. You are building a relationship of trust, not one of war.

You can make contact again **before** three months have elapsed if you wish, but contact and recontact your two hundred or so prospects without fail at least once within that ninety-day period.

If you follow this schedule and move daily through your list whether you reach the party or not, you will need to average only three to four calls per day. If you don't reach a particular prospect after two attempts, give up phoning until the next three-month cycle unless you have something really important to say now, in which case you keep on trying.

Instead create a relationship by sending a handwritten note saying: "Sorry that I missed you. If I may, I'll be in touch within three months." Enclose your business card and be in touch again, within three months or less.

If you do not get through next time, send another note and another and another, until you do get through. (See section on "Saying thank you in a memorable way" for advice on the type and quality of card on which to write your note.)

> *"There is no human problem which could not be solved if people would simply do as I advise."* Gore Vidal

The first cycle

In my experience, the first time you make the rounds of your contacts, you usually get some business. There are always firms that are unhappy with their existing supplier and will say yes just to establish a new relationship.

However, in general you'll find that your chances of getting an appointment from the first cold letter or phone call are about one-half to one per cent. So, from two hundred prospects, you might get one or two appointments the first time around.

To all those who say "No", you will say, "Thank you" and also, "If you don't mind, we'll be in touch again in three months' time." Don't be discouraged; just as life changes, so does business. When needs change and your product or service is required, you will be favoured over the casual cold caller because your prospect has grown to trust you. That means you get the business. Prospects don't mean "No"; they mean "Not now".

The second cycle

Within three months, you write and/or phone again, just as you said you would. Your percentage of appointments is likely to rise to about two or three per cent—maybe a total of six appointments from your two hundred contacts.

The third cycle

Three months later, at the ninth month, write and/or phone again. Now, because you have been in regular contact, the prospect has learned to trust you. You didn't give up the first or second time: you came back. In the third cycle, your appointments are likely to rise to around seven per cent—perhaps fourteen or more appointments from the two hundred prospects.

The fourth cycle and onward

Beginning with the fourth cycle, the percentages tend to increase dramatically and you may find about thirty per cent of your prospects will agree to an appointment. Be prepared for success: by the fifth cycle, you can get appointments with up to sixty per cent of your contacts.

My figures about the percentage of positive responses you get in each cycle are on the conservative side. People often tell me that they get a level of response higher than my predictions. If you're able to do better, terrific!

However, start off comfortably, assuming you will do as well as this model suggests. Fewer positive responses may be a sign that you have to change or improve the look or sound of your message, or that you need a stronger, more frequent effort to maintain a regular stream of prospects.

A little research is enough

> *"Great moments in science: Einstein discovers that time is actually money."* Gary Larson cartoon caption

Entrepreneurs often paralyse themselves by doing too much research. They sit around for hours, days, weeks, tracking down what they consider to be relevant information about an organisation, using the research as an excuse not to pick up that phone.

In essence, most of the research is a waste of time because whatever information you can gather is usually out of date by the time you get it.

All that "knowledge" can set you up for a bad appointment, because prospects love to talk about themselves, and if you go to a meeting full of information, you may not listen. You may be presupposing and presuming and you may even be bored with everything the prospect is going to tell you.

A small amount of research is enough, something that might take you a couple of hours, such as phoning to request an annual report, and then reading it.

Simply call a gatekeeper and say, "Would you mind helping me? I'm trying to get a little more information about your company. Could you send me a copy of your annual report?"

For privately held companies, ask for brochures and any other information they distribute. Use this opportunity to build a relationship with the gatekeeper and when the annual report and brochures you requested are received, call back or write a note to say thank you.

When you arrive for your meeting, your prospect will be aware that you've done some homework. Then ask intelligent questions and listen with genuine interest.

Don't ever be afraid of cold calling. After the first successful contact, your prospects become warm calls.

Take time out to make the Saatchi & Saatchi canal system work for you

> *"Do it big or stay in bed."* Opera producer Larry Kelly

Review your list of around two hundred prospects. It is possible that you did not get two hundred. The reason most people give is that they "know" many of their likely prospects have a long history of being tied to another company, so their prospect numbers dropped back considerably. May I suggest that you put these people back on your list. You will never know until you try whether a prospect is going to become a client. Everything changes. Even the most committed business relationship can fail for all the usual reasons that personal relationships fail.

Get ready to make the canal system really work. One of my clients put aside Friday afternoons to work everything out. His prospect list grew a little longer every Friday until he got his two hundred.

All the information was in the computer, he had a modem so that the phone numbers were dialled at the push of a button, a large box of good-looking cards was at his side for those "Sorry that I missed you when I rang" notes. He was determined not to do too much research and to make at least four to six calls a day.

And it worked. He told me he made a second call to a prospect, three months later, and she said to please come in, he was the only person that had ever called back when he said he would. So it doesn't take much to be ahead of the game.

Those note-cards are of key importance. Playing telephone tag is frustrating. By handwriting a note and sending it off each time you cannot contact the prospect, you "shift the monkey" right out of the way. Otherwise you end up with so many calls to do you feel tempted to give up.

> *"I have a new philosophy. I am only going to dread one day at a time."* Charles Schulz

Why are we so afraid to make cold calls? The fear of rejection? We don't want to spoil our day by doing things which might not work. You bet!

All that is needed to overcome the distaste of making cold calls is a slightly different perspective: the view that new-business development is a numbers game.

So, if we have two hundred contacts, we know that somewhere out there is somebody who's going to say "yes". We just have to get there by way of a lot of "No, not now".

Cold calling

> *"If called by a panther, don't anther."* Ogden Nash, (1902–1971)

As Saatchi's David Miln says, "Those who make three times more phone calls than their competitors are four times more successful."

Considering that almost no-one consistently makes new-business phone calls, being three times better than your competitors is easy!

Everyone experiences ups and downs in business. If you get appointments with your first few phone calls, you may think, "This is easy, anyone can do new business".

Then you go into a long, low time when all you hear are those deadly excuses: every person you call is busy, is interstate, on holidays, out of the office, in a meeting, will call you back, or simply does not want to see you.

Get over the pain by getting back on the phone, trotting along like a marathon runner, just getting the "Yes, please come in" or the "No, not now". Yesses and noes are the prospects' choice. They will say "yes" to you when they are ready.

The longer, harder and smarter you work, the luckier you get. In London it was said that business was done two months of the year, but no-one knew which two months. In New York getting appointments was so tough it was the equivalent of winning the war in the Middle East.

Then I found out that in New York business was done one month of the year: in August when "everyone" was out of town. Those who were left behind were delighted to see people. Outside of New York, everyone was willing to see you . . . but then one had to travel in order to reach them and that was impressive enough to get you the appointment. In Australia and South Africa it seems to be year-round business—with exceptions such as the end of the financial year, school holidays and Christmas/New Year. And although I find appointments relatively easy to get in South Africa, the decisions take just as long as they do everywhere else in the world.

In Hong Kong I found business was done every hour of every day, except in August when the European side of business went quiet with the expatriates away on holidays. Other than that, business went on as normal, night and day. And in the end, why do people buy? Because of greed, fear and laziness. If you can meet one or all of those needs, you will likely have a quicker decision.

How do you get going?

> *"The two hardest things to handle in life are failure and success."* Unknown

First of all, you must develop a contact card, or have all the information on the computer screen:

Name and title of the person you're calling
Name of this person's gatekeeper (if you don't know it, find out)
Correct company name and address
Correct telephone and fax numbers
Company's industry
Company's size by staff and revenue

From research you should also have:

(a) The knowledge to choose a wide band of likely prospects, all of whom will one day need your product or service. The Commonality Survey is your guideline here.

(b) The "single-minded proposition"—the reason your clients

chose you and stay with you, so that you can clearly tell your prospects the one major benefit of choosing to use your product or service.

No need to confuse them—just give them one valid reason, from their point of view, why they should meet with you.

Remember, they won't give up their time to discuss their needs with you unless they can foresee a major benefit.

Take the card in your hand or bring up the information on your computer screen and dial the phone number. Ask to speak to the person whom you have identified as the top decision maker in the organisation. It is easy to work down through an organisation, but it is extremely difficult to work up.

It is always best to write to and ask for one of the top titles: chairman, president, chief executive officer, chief financial officer. If you're later told to call someone further down the organisational hierarchy, at least you've made contact with a senior executive to whom you can refer.

Try to enlist the gatekeeper's help. If you have mailed a letter and information, enquire whether your mailing has been received. If there is no memory of it, remail the package, but addressed to the gatekeeper personally, for the attention of the boss. Wait several days, call the gatekeeper again and say, "Did you receive our package?"

At this point, of course, the gatekeeper will remember it. Ask, "Have you been able to pass it on yet? Do you know when (the boss) would like to meet with me?"

The incidence of appointments after remailing and enlisting the help of the gatekeeper is often very high, providing you have a simple way of explaining what your product or service will do for them . . . what is unique about you.

Another valuable technique is to get the name of the gatekeeper and fax that person for their boss, explaining that you will be in the area at a certain time on a certain day and will visit unless it is inconvenient for them.

You will always get a response as they don't want you turning up if they are not going to be there, particularly if you are travelling interstate to see them. If the time is not convenient you can negotiate another mutually suitable time. Now you have an appointment around which to base your next visit to the area.

To make your mailing package memorable, use simple design techniques. For IMCOR in New York I took their ordinary large white envelopes and had them overprinted with a broad, royal blue stripe down the left-hand side. When we asked if our mailing package had been received and described it, the result was instant recognition and helpfulness.

Inside the envelope was a royal blue folder and cream letterhead with IMCOR in gold foil. The supporting information was done on cream paper with—yes, you've guessed it—a royal blue line down the side. We got a lot of comments about the integrated and professional look of our mailing piece and a lot of appointments, too.

Cold calls can be the best part of your day

> *"The trouble with using experience as a guide is that the final exam often comes first and then the lesson."*
>
> Unknown

Learn to like cold calling. You would die of exhaustion if everyone said "yes" to an appointment: I ask people to physically leap up and say,"Hurrah, I got a 'no', now I don't have to go out in the rain/cold/heat/noise . . ." and really mean it.

You can also moan and groan when you get a "yes" if you like, because now you do have to go out in the rain/cold/heat/noise etc.

See cold calling as the easiest part of your day. With this system, cold calling is simple because if people are not in, you simply write a note and keep moving. To increase your chances of a personal contact, start early in the day, around eight o'clock. You will often find people in between twelve and one in the afternoon and between five and six in the evening.

Remember to use the fax and enrol the gatekeeper when you really want an appointment. You can speak to the gatekeeper, ask permission to send a fax, explain your reasons for needing the appointment, list your free times and continue to liaise with this key person.

You may never speak to the senior person until the day of the appointment, but you will surely get it organised.

Look good to yourself when you're making phone calls. With more and more people working from home, the temptation can be to dress down for the occasion.

Try this for a test. One morning dress in your best business outfit and start making calls. Then change to an old tracksuit and see if you feel as great.

Any sense of self-worth comes out in your voice; similarly, any self-doubt.

Understanding the person on the other end of the phone

(My thanks to British Telecom for their notes from which this section is taken.)

> *"It takes a great person to be a good listener."*
> Arthur Helps (1813–1875)

Most people fall into one of four personal styles. Each of these types requires a different response from you if you are to be successful in getting appointments.

However, don't be too quick to judge people by how they sound on the phone. There are too many unknown elements to a phone conversation: you cannot see the other person and you don't know what kind of day he or she has had.

Stay relaxed and listen; allow an image of the speaker to drift into your mind. You will find that such an impression can often prove remarkably accurate.

For instance, allowing for regional variations, a rapid rate of rational speech generally shows above-average intelligence. Hesitation, stammering and pauses may suggest anxiety or indecisiveness, or that you are talking to the wrong person. Generally, you will be able to figure out how to conduct your conversation by using language that fits with the following four personality styles: Aspirers, Admirers, Enquirers and Inspirers.

Listening for the language

> *"I never know how much of what I say is true."*
> Bette Midler

Aspirers use the language of achievement and are often entrepreneurs in their own business. They speak about setting goals, working towards objectives, planning and thinking ahead, making progress and moving onward.

Their tone is brisk, businesslike and purposeful. They will finish your sentences, interrupt you and end the call abruptly. Don't assume they are in the office when you speak to them. They could well be at home, in a car, on a train or a plane. They are forever moving around, setting their goals and going forward.

Aspirers want callers to be brisk, direct, organised and straight to the point. If you waste their time, you will be unpopular. Have a clear idea of what you want from the call before phoning.

Stress how your ideas can help Aspirers to attain goals or make more efficient use of their time. Don't bother them with details.

Give the whole picture, prices, benefits and availability in one quick statement. If you follow up by fax, electronic or voice mail, you will impress them.

Show yourself to be quick, accurate and efficient. If they like your style, you'll get their business.

Enquirers act like accountants (and often are), saying things like: "Let's consider the facts . . .", "Speaking objectively . . .", "Logical thinking requires . . .", "The way I see it . . .", and "I think it is important that we do it this way".

They speak slowly, reflecting carefully on their words and instantly correcting any mistakes they consider you've made.

They let ideas sink in for a long time before they reply and before they commit themselves, leaving you to face long silences.

Enquirers do not like social chat. Just provide relevant facts and figures. If you don't know the answer, say so immediately and honestly—don't guess.

Say you'll find out, say you'll phone back. Speak firmly, unemotionally, clearly and precisely.

It's a good idea to send Enquirers a fax or letter covering all the key points in your conversations, so that they continue to be impressed by your efficiency. When Enquirers have enough facts, they will trust you with just one project, not an entire job. When you've proved yourself, you will get the job.

Admirers are often found in human resources roles and use phrases like "My feeling about this is . . .", or "My intuition tells me that . . .", or "I sense that . . ." They speak quietly and calmly.

They listen carefully to what you say. There may be sudden long silences that make you think that the phone has broken down. It hasn't; they're just quietly and genuinely listening to you. Their preferred role in an organisation is in human resources.

Admirers want business calls to be sociable. They like to chat about friends, families, holidays, sports or the weather. Take time to listen to their ideas or problems and be warm and caring about them. Admirers use their silences to coax you into revealing information about yourself, your business and your feelings—perhaps even more than you may have intended to tell them.

When they are sure that you are "one of them" and they determine that your service will benefit the people in their organisation, you will get their business.

Inspirers are visionaries and often heads of large organisations. They love words that convey great energy. They say things like "It sounds great ...", "This is an amazing project ...", "I am delighted by the idea ...", "You're going to love this". They will cut you short when they get bored with the conversation. Their closing phrases are words like "Fine, fine ...", "Right ...", "Okay ...", when they mean "Goodbye".

They talk quickly and urgently, with ideas tumbling excitedly over one another, such is their speed of delivery. Being at the top in a big way, they hate detail, but love big pictures. Inspirers get bored quickly. They need variety in conversations; so don't be afraid of introducing several different topics or jumping from one idea to the next.

Speak in a lively, enthusiastic manner that conveys urgency and excitement about what you're doing.

Inspirers also respond with delight to a "thank you" expressed in a quick note or a simple phone call. Keep Inspirers entertained and you will have their business.

Talking to the senior executive

> *"Nobody can make you feel inferior without your consent."* Eleanor Roosevelt (1884–1962)

Sometimes you will get straight through to the senior executive with whom you want to speak, often if you phone between 8 and 9 a.m., at lunch time or after 5 p.m. If you're not prepared, you may be left thinking, "Help! I didn't mean to speak to this person. I meant to have a long, ongoing relationship with the secretary to save me from an appointment I'm rather nervous about."

If it happens that you get to speak directly with someone who says, "Yes, I got your package and, yes, I do want to see you," be ready to respond appropriately. Negotiate a suitable time; write or fax immediately so that the person has it in writing. Call the day before to confirm. I call again on the day itself to reconfirm, as often something has come up to delay the other person—and a useless journey is saved.

It is over to you to probe gently, focusing on their needs. Do not try to respond with instant-fix answers. After the meeting, remember to say and to write thank you to everyone who helped you and saw you. The important thing is to send off your note of thanks as soon as possible after the day of the appointment, preferably that evening or at the latest, the next day.

Within three to five days of the meeting, you should, as promised, come back with some suggestions on how your company can help, having given real time to thinking the answers through. From the prospect's point of view, you have behaved well every step of the way. You have kept in touch before and after the meeting, you have come back with some well-thought-out recommendations within the promised time scale.

How many other people will they have met who behave in such a quality way? After all, quality service is only doing exactly what you say you will do within the time frame agreed on.

Where I am dealing with a large number of assistants in an organisation, I draw a rough chart in my diary of where everyone sits, their names and who they report to. Then when I go in, I know which person does what and where to find them.

Getting the spelling of their names right is very important. One that I spend time with is Karin as opposed to the more usual spelling of Karen. If I were to get the spelling wrong on a thank-you note, it would really wreck my best efforts. Another instance: recently, after someone in London was very helpful, I wrote to thank him and later phoned to tell him the positive result of his introduction.

He commented that my letter was in his, "Nice letter file, that has remarkably few in it". I know that he does a great deal for people, so why so few "thank you" notes? It takes but a few minutes, but is remembered forever.

Make a first pass at identifying some people you know by their phone styles

> *"When ideas fail, words come in handy."* Goethe

Talking their language is easy when you know how and what to look for. Make a first try at identifying prospects and clients by their personality types, using the information you have just read about telephone style and language. See if you can write in the name of at least one person after each of the following styles:

Aspirer (entrepreneurial type)

....

Enquirer (chief financial officer type)

....

Admirer (human resources type)

....

Inspirer (visionary, head of large corporation type)

....

Secrets of good phoning

> *"For people who like peace and quiet: a phoneless cord."*
> Unknown

When you are feeling anxious, the tension can come through in your voice and create problems for you on the phone. Research shows that an anxious man sounds elderly, inflexible, irritable, bad-tempered. Tense women can be judged to be irrational, emotional and unstable.

You can get rid of tension before you phone, by relaxing your mind and your muscles. Take a deep breath, tighten up all over, clench your fists and toes, stretch your legs and hold for a slow count of five.

Relax and breathe out for a count of five. Take another deep breath, hold for a count of five, breathe out and relax. Make sure that your teeth are unclenched by putting your tongue against the back of your top front teeth.

Continue to breathe quietly: five seconds in, and five seconds out. Feel a deep, calm relaxation flowing through your whole body. Concentrate on your breathing—in for five, out for five. Soothe yourself by picturing yourself doing something relaxing that you love doing.

Above all else, when making your call, care about the person at the other end. Be polite and respectful. Always keep in mind the four types of professionals with whom you may be dealing. Avoid wasting the other person's time, or on the other hand, not spending enough time for the other individual to feel comfortable with you.

Staying in control

> *"Experience teaches you to recognise a mistake when you have made it again."* Unknown

There are powerful ways of staying in control of a call. One way to sound more authoritative is to stand up while phoning. When you stand up, your whole system is more aroused and alert, your sense of power is heightened and your mind is sharpened. A smile will make you sound affirmative, bright and happy.

Smiling is a good tactic to use when you are talking to Aspirers, who can be intimidating by the rapidity and brusqueness of their speech. Conversely, not smiling can make you sound flat, dull and tired. Not at all a pleasure to talk to.

On the other hand, if you're after an appointment to sell a holiday in the sun and you want to sound relaxed and casual, there is no harm in lounging back in your chair and chatting with an Admirer or an Inspirer as though you were sitting on the beach.

Effective listening

> *"If the phone doesn't ring, it's me."*
> Song title by Jimmy Buffet

Earlier we looked at design techniques and saw that it was important to decide whether to position your copy on the left- or right-hand side of the page in order to send the desired message to the reader. Similarly, it makes a difference whether you listen to a caller with your right ear or your left, believe it or not!

Listen with your right ear to evaluate complicated facts, because the right ear communicates with the cool, analytical left side of your brain.

Right-ear listening is helpful when you speak with an Aspirer or an Enquirer, to understand information correctly and respond logically.

To listen sympathetically, hold the phone to your left ear. This transmits information to the right side of your brain, the hemisphere of intuition, imagination and creativity. By increasing sensitivity to unspoken emotions, left-ear listening enhances empathy. Admirers and Inspirers generally listen with their left ears, and should be heard with your left ear, because they are attuned to emotions.

There are two main barriers to effective listening. The first is distraction: doing two complicated tasks at the same time, such as reading while you are taking a call.

Decide priorities. If the memo is more urgent, read it before you get on the phone. Otherwise, you will listen only to the first few words and then concentrate on the reading. The second barrier is dismissive listening, which occurs when someone has a problem and because we are not pleased with what we are hearing, we want to interrupt.

To avoid this, attend not only to the spoken words but also to those left unsaid. Say as little as possible while you are listening. Encourage the other person to continue.

Murmur phrases like "I see", or "I understand", or "That's interesting", or "Do tell me more". Thus, the speaker feels welcome to speak freely.

Keep your feelings to yourself for the moment. Don't get angry and dismiss what the person is saying by responding too soon. Wait until you've heard everything; take notes, and pinpoint the critical issues.

Then come back calmly and quietly when you've both had a chance to get to the root of the problem. The right time to express your side of the argument is after you've listened long enough to understand the other person's problem exactly.

Don't take the issue personally. You are only sorry about it; you didn't cause it.

As a case in point, IMCOR in New York upgraded their computers. After a few days' use, they crashed, causing a great deal of distress and loss of updated documents.

Among the losses were recent changes to this book, painstakingly marked up by my editor and keyed in by my assistant during some late nights at the office.

Unknowingly, I happily returned what I thought was the most recent version. Her phone call to me made it very clear that a great deal of her editing had not been done and she was justifiably upset.

Now in the old days I would have become defensive and upset, too. This time I just murmured along and agreed that it was an incredible waste of her time and hard work.

Later I found out what had happened and we were able to discuss it amicably. I was sorry about it, but I didn't cause it. A good aid to effective listening is to check your understanding by feeding back key points at suitable moments. Say, "So you're suggesting that ...", or "Then we agree that ...". Checking important points prevents much wasted effort and encourages you to take good notes as the conversation proceeds.

Head your notes with the date and time of the call and the caller's name, phone number, title and company. You have a record of what went on by doing no more than stapling your notes together and putting them into your file.

Take time to write a letter or memo that confirms your understanding of the discussion and what you have both agreed to do next. Mail, fax or deliver it as soon as you can after the discussion. The longer you wait, the less the recipient trusts your notes as their memory has gone dim, too.

Saying goodbye

> *"Most of our future lies ahead."* Denny Crum, American football coach

We have all seen it: colleagues holding the phone at arm's length and making winding motions with their other arm. The person at the other end is just not going to hang up.

Being caught on the phone is a sign that you have lost control of the conversation. Ending your call efficiently is as important as starting it correctly.

It is unlikely that you will ever get a long goodbye from **Aspirers** (the entrepreneur type), because they are in such a hurry to hang up. If you do want to say goodbye first, put the reason for ending the call firmly back into the other person's zone.

Say, "Thank you for your time. I won't keep you any longer because I know you're busy."

Bring a conversation with **Enquirers** (accountant types) to a suitable conclusion by promising to send them a fax or letter to confirm your conversation.

They are happy when they know the substance will be available in black and white. They can put it into the file and cover themselves against any possible problems.

Admirers (human resources types) hate to be cut short. They see it as a form of rejection. Don't sound as though it is goodbye forever. Say, "It has been nice talking to you. Speak to you again soon."

Inspirers (visionaries) are far less sensitive to hasty goodbyes. Being bored so easily, they always want to rush off to something new. Say something like "I must dash", and you will be talking their language.

When dealing with a relative stranger, be polite. Use the person's name in your final sentence, but be hesitant to use the first name unless you have been invited to do so. It is better to be thought of as very polite rather than too pushy and friendly.

Say, "Thank you, Ms Jones, I will send you a fax," or "Thank you, Mr Smith, I will be in touch."

If there is some information you particularly want remembered, repeat it immediately before saying goodbye. We often remember what people said at the beginning and at the end, but we may not recall what they said in the middle. Do not be diverted into a difficult discussion. If someone wants information that you cannot give at present, such as more precise costs or details, say something like, "I don't have that information at hand at present, but I shall find it and get back to you".

Why are you making the call?

Always keep in mind the purpose of your call. Remember that your first phone call to an organisation is not to sell; you are only setting up an appointment. The first rule of cold calling is, "Never sell over the phone".

People will of course say,"Why should I see you?" and instead of selling to them, use your single-minded proposition. If you worked for Minolta, for instance, you could use their statement so clearly expressed on their billboard. You could simply say, "Because we understand the office".

The listener's brain is going to do one of two things—he is either going to think that his office is perfect and he does not need you, or his office could do with some help—and an appointment might be a very good idea. You are not selling on the first phone call—you are simply letting them decide whether they do or do not want to meet with you.

You have to build a relationship and identify needs before you can sell, so all you are seeking is an appointment to meet. That's all you want at this stage, just the opportunity to meet and identify the other's needs. Then if you can help, after considered time on their issues and what it is that you have to offer, you can start selling.

If the answer is "no" to an appointment, thank them and remind them that you will be calling back within three months. (Remember "no" means "no not now," not "no for ever".)

Recently I got a "no" and was advised that the company had just taken on another consultant and named him. I accepted it at the time, but knowing that the other consultant and I were complementary rather than similar in what we did, I rang back and repitched. I got the appointment and the business.

Later, when I was introduced to the team that I was to train, the Managing Director stated that I was a living example of my philosophy that "no" means "no not now," not "no forever". So be grateful for the "no" answers.

Why? Because you couldn't handle appointments with all of your two hundred or so prospects at the same time, anyway—you would die from exhaustion! When they say "yes", it will be because they do really want to see you.

Make cold calls work for you (have fun on the phone!)
First, let's address the subject of rejection. "Why this fear of calling back?" I asked myself. I remembered as children that we never took no for an answer, we simply nagged until we got what we wanted—be it an ice cream or a skateboard or whatever was the "in" thing at the time.

I now call this the ice cream theory. You ask for an ice cream and the answer is no. You nag and keep on nagging and ten years later you have had a thousand ice creams. So when did we start believing that no meant no forever? When did rejection start to hurt so much?

I recalled my teenage years when I first thought that no was forever. All dressed up and excited to be going to my first school dance—ready to dance with my first boyfriend, all night. Only he danced with someone else all night, and I was alone against the wall. For the first time I knew the meaning of total rejection, the awful fear of not being wanted.

When I ask a group if this has happened to any of them, everyone in the group agrees that they have had a similar experience and it too made them afraid of "no".

We have to revert to childhood, when "no" was simply the signal to bide our time until it was "yes".

Now that we know why we fear rejection, let's accept (again) that it is okay for people to say "no not now"—and let's set out to get some "yes" answers by staying in touch until we do. Since good phone calls are great one-act plays, use all these techniques to please your prospect or client and entertain yourself:

Dress well to feel good. This really makes a difference. Those of us who have a home office will readily agree that we feel and sound much more empowered when we take a phone call in our power suits on the way to a meeting than we do when we are just back from walking the dogs.

Stand up to sound powerful, smile to sound happy, pace your delivery to match that of the person you are speaking to. Look for clues as to their personality style—are they an Aspirer, Enquirer, Admirer, Inspirer? Adapt to their style and make their day a happier one for having heard from you.

Think back to when you were a child and knew instinctively what sort of mood the adults were in. You had only to walk into the room or hear their voices to know whether it was a good day or a bad one for them.

The same thing can be picked up on the phone, usually by the way in which people say hello. There may be a certain tightness in their voice. Regardless of whether you pick up that clue, always ask people at every level of the organisation if it is a good time for them to speak to you.

I usually say, "Good morning, Paul, it's Wendy Evans speaking. Can you talk now, or have I caught you at a bad time?" or if I know the person better: "Hi Ros, it's Wendy . . . is it okay for you to speak now?"

In my whole phone-answering life, only one person has ever consistently done that to me—and am I grateful! That person is Stephen Hickmore of "The Search Advantage" in South Africa. Stephen specialises in finding staff for the hospitality industry and has my undying respect for this simple courtesy. It reminds me to do it more often!

The reason is that not everyone has a gatekeeper and not every gatekeeper is at their desk when you phone. People can often be in a meeting in their offices when you ring. The simple courtesy of checking if it is convenient to speak now will always win you points. You will readily be given another time to call back if you ask quickly but politely. You could say something like, "Just give me a time that is convenient and I'll call back then."

Write notes as you talk and make sure that as details or decisions change during the conversation, you update the notes. If your notes are clear and you confirm the key points, you do not have to struggle to remember them at a later date. A click of the stapler and you have a good rough record of the conversation for your file.

When you note an appointment in your diary, fill in all the details, including the address and phone number of the person and company you are going to see.

Then if you are running late, you have one source that is always full of correct detail: your diary. A flip of the page and you can make that quick call to notify the person of the delay.

Saying thank you in a memorable way

> *"The brain is a wonderful organ; it starts working the moment you get up in the morning and does not stop until you get to the office."* Robert Frost (1874–1963)

As we said earlier, always write to thank everyone who has helped you: the person who sent you the company's annual report and promotional literature, the gatekeeper who helped you get the appointment, the person you met with and anyone else in the organisation who referred you.

Tell those who were not at the meeting how it went, thank them, and if another action has resulted, write to tell them how that turned out.

Think how often you have helped other people and how—sometimes? often?—the silence afterwards was deafening.

Vary your thanks. It is all too easy to send a typed note on company letterhead. All that is required is a signature, an envelope and a stamp. There must be many millions of these going around the world daily, achieving little in the way of impact.

You can make sure your "thank you" will be remembered if you do it in a way that shows you really noticed the kindness and assistance received: you can send a handwritten note-card.

If you are not sure that your handwriting is easy to read, use a calligraphy pen instead. Practise the calligraphy strokes with the help of the instruction leaflet. The improvement will be extraordinary. The pens can be bought at any stationers. Be sure to get one with a refillable bladder, not just the small plastic cartridges that run out quickly.

Buy good quality ink in a businesslike colour such as blue or blue-black. Pure black looks a little grim for thankyou notes. Do not get into different colours such as brown or green, as they are not acceptable in business.

Lately I have found felt-tipped calligraphy pens and they are the best. But be sure to buy several at a time because they suddenly run out.

Look around for memorable note-cards, the kind that are blank inside. You can find these at a bookstore or a museum or art gallery bookshop. Make sure they look so attractive that people will hesitate to throw them in the wastepaper basket.

I found some Japanese lacquer screen cards in black and gold at the Metropolitan Museum in New York. They cost no more than other quite ordinary cards but looked much more special. Even a year later, these cards were still on display when I visited certain offices.

Keep a big box of your memorable cards close by. Try to choose cards that appeal to both men and women or have a box of each. Make sure the cards are congruent with the image of your company you want people to receive. A few minutes and a few cards later, you will have added considerably to your clients' and prospects' memories of your meeting.

The moment you feel a "thank you" is due, handwrite a greeting card and send it off with your business card. It's like paying your bills. You get a wonderful feeling of: "I've done it and it's out of the way."

And remember that you can use this practice with prospects and clients when you have been unable to reach them by phone, just to say, "Sorry I missed you, I'll be in touch within three months."

Consider sending postcards to clients and warm prospects when you are away on business or on holidays. I send one to the client and one to the gatekeeper, with my contact details and the date of return. I will already have given the details to both, but a bright card has more impact and is easier to find than the original note. To prospects the message is more simple: "I am away, but will be in contact when I get back."

Do you find it difficult to say "thank you" in a way that shows genuine appreciation? It can be as difficult to say "thank you" in a sincere way as it is to leave a message on an answering machine. Those of us who are usually competent with business language sometimes disintegrate when we have to write a card or leave a clear message on a machine.

Nevertheless, it is important to personalise your "thank you" and it's not difficult to do if you use this simple technique: set up a mental picture of the person you're going to contact and prepare a message as though that person were standing in front of you.

Now it will be easier for you to look at her or him and say or write, "You were very kind and I appreciated your time and patience. Thank you for your help." Or even, "Thanks, you were great. Much appreciated."

Use this technique every time you have to write, be it a thank-you card, letter, brochure, flyer, or a company's "address to the nation". By having a clear picture of that one person whom you most want to hear the message, you come across as a genuine person—which you are, as you are not trying to communicate with the whole world, just with that one important person.

Your style is your own, your message is for them and they feel it, hear it and see it as a real communication.

I was fortunate to attend a Saatchi & Saatchi "creative week" where we asked one of the stars how he created a global campaign. Andy replied that he certainly did **not** try to put in a black cow, a white sheep, a brown dog. Or a redhead, a blonde and a brunette. Or even a man, a woman and a child.

He quite simply sat down to create something that was absolutely perfect for him. When he was satisfied, there was every chance that other people around the world would love it, too.

Ever since that workshop, I too have sat down to create for myself and just one other person, who represents the buyer. If I am writing about a product for a mother and baby, I get to know well just one mother and baby—and write to them. Then there is every chance that other mothers and babies will hear me, too.

This way you shift the "monkeys" off your back: the gibbering voices that call at you to please the boss, the client, the marketplace, your parents, your family, your friends. When these monkeys rule you, you please no-one, not even yourself. Get rid of them and you please yourself and the world.

A further tip: never start a letter or card with the words "Thank you", because when people see those opening words, they think they have got the whole message.

By leaving the thanks until last, you force them to read all the words in case there are other things they ought to know. And there may well be, as you might be reconfirming a further appointment or providing them with some details they had requested.

> *"Success didn't spoil me, I have always been insufferable."*
> Fran Lebowitz

Make note-cards work for you

Think about the pleasure you get at Christmas and birthdays when you open the mailbox and find caring messages from people you like. Perhaps you can communicate with your clients in a way that makes it clear your response is meant for them as individuals. For example:

You're a doctor; you've just seen a new patient and prescribed a likely cure. Consider sending a "Get well" card and following up with a phone call to see how the patient is doing.

You're a travel agent whose customers are on their way back from a trip you arranged. Send a "Welcome home" card and ask them to call and tell you about their experiences. If they do not phone you (being busy on their return, they probably won't), be sure to phone them.

You run a hotel and new clients were big spenders in the bars and restaurants. You can be fairly sure, by their joyous disregard for sleep or cost and their delight in having fun, that they are Inspirers. Inspirers love a thank you and recognition.

So mail a "Thank you for staying with us" card to their business address. Put a note inside and ask them to let you know when a return trip is planned so that you can put a special gift in their rooms.

Give them three gift choices and arrange for their selection to be in their rooms before arrival. Upgrade them to a better room, if they have not already booked the most expensive suite. You will more than get your money back in their expenditure in the restaurants and bars, as this personality type always returns a favour. Perhaps they will enjoy the experience so much that you will hear from their friends as well.

Why not send birthday cards to everyone who has ever stayed with you, as does the Peninsula Hotel in Hong Kong? For years I have heard about and seen these birthday cards. I now think it is probably the single most successful ongoing promotion I have come across, because it really suits a grand hotel to remember people in this way.

Birthday cards can apply to whatever industry you're in. If you're in insurance, send a birthday card on the date of the policy renewal; if you are selling cars or real estate, send a birthday card on the date the owner bought the car, house or building. This practice is fun and different—and that makes you memorable.

Again, never delay sending your thanks. The closer your note is to the action, the more powerful the effect of a "thank you" on the person who contributed.

Think back—and make thank you cards your "policy" now and forever

> *"It's fun being in the same decade as you."*
> Franklin Delano Roosevelt in a letter to Winston Churchill, 1942

Think back over the past month. Did anyone do anything for you that was kind, helpful or considerate, that you now feel was worthy of a thank you note—but you didn't send one? Could writing a note now come more easily, realising that it makes you virtually unique in this marketplace? For the cost of a card and a postage stamp you become memorable. I mean a postage stamp, not a swift pass through the franking machine.

Mark the envelope "personal", address it as neatly as you can, put a proper stamp on, and it will slip straight through to the recipient's desk. Your card will give pleasure that day and you will be remembered for sending it.

Recently I received two personal notes, one to say "thank you" for a lunch and the other from a dentist. Both were handwritten. The first was a very elegant card. The second was a note on company letterhead welcoming me to his practice. The card is up on the bookshelf, the dentist's company letterhead is sadly in the bin.

While I was enormously impressed that the dentist sent me a handwritten note, it is hard to put it anywhere but in the bin. Not so with the card. Grab the occasion to send cards that people will display and so remember you constantly.

Key points to remember

Develop an outstanding corporate sound. Ring your own company and hear how your staff handle enquiries. Look upon your phone calls to clients and prospects as one-act plays designed to give them pleasure, thereby benefiting you.

Never sell on the first phone call; the first call is only to set up an appointment. Remember to use your single-minded proposition as to why they should give you the appointment. Always start with the head of any corporation with which you want to do business. You can get passed down an organisation but not up.

Say "thank you" in a memorable way. Always send a card when thanks are due. Use cards also to say, "Sorry I missed you". Use cards to invite, to remind, or just to say "hi". Make sure the card matches the corporate image you display and always put in your business card.

All over the world, people have said to me that they have contacted everyone once and have not liked to go back because they did not know what to say next. I had exactly the same experience when I represented the Peninsula Hotel Group Hong Kong as their regional sales manager in Australia.

I called on the whole of the travel industry, distributed brochures and price lists for the many Peninsula Group properties in Asia, got lots of commitment to using the hotels and then nothing much happened!

The sales manager at Cathay Pacific (where I had my office) told me to go back and do the same thing all over again. I did, it worked and that is what I now recommend. Do the same thing over and over again until the message gets through. Step eight will help you do that.

Step Eight

The regular follow-up

"There is no they, only us."	Bumper sticker

Defend your right to be absolutely consistent—even to the point of being boring (but only to yourself).

Of the hundreds, perhaps thousands of people who phone your prospects, you are probably the only one who is making contact every ninety days or less. You come across as serious and committed. You want the prospect's business, and you have proved it by staying in touch. They can't help but think if you manage your business this well, imagine what you could do for them.

What to say next

You may be wondering why, if it's as simple as consistent contact, everyone's business isn't growing by leaps and bounds.

The fact is that most people think they have said everything after the first round of mailing and phoning and they don't know what to do next. So often nothing further is done.

There is a tendency to think that the prospects will ring in when they need something. That doesn't very often happen! The simple truth is that you must stay in contact and say the same thing the second, third, fourth and fifth time and ever after, but with minor variations. The good news is that sixty per cent of all sales opportunities arrive after the fifth contact.

At about fifteen months of contacting in three-month cycles, appointments will begin to come in droves. When I returned to New York to follow up on IMCOR's success, they were on their fifth three-month cycle of contacting eight thousand prospects America-wide. As I arrived they said, "Just as you promised, we are overwhelmed with success, exactly on the fifteenth month, and yes, we are having trouble keeping up!"

Mind you, I can be wrong—it can happen *sooner*, depending on the product, the promotion and the market demand. Recently two women, who are friends, both left their jobs in insurance to become self-employed. They visited another friend, Maureen, and expressed their concern that although they had an idea, they didn't know how to get started.

She, knowing me, had my book conveniently on the table beside them and said, "Read this". Which they did for two days and nights and then went into their secretarial placement and temp business.

When they saw Maureen next they said, "Tell Wendy Evans she is wrong. It doesn't take 15 months—we were in profit in the first month." I don't mind being wrong for that kind of happy beginning.

Which brings me to another important issue: that of choosing the business that you go into. First you must choose something that you have a passion for. Without passion you won't be up and at it with any degree of energy.

Secondly, don't, if you can possibly avoid it, start up a business which no-one has ever heard of before. It takes a great deal of time and energy and money to invent and present a brand-new product and there is little guarantee of success. Having a great new idea is likely to be more exciting to you than it is to anyone else.

Try to have a great similar idea. For example I met a man who had opened up a pharmacy in the walkway to one of the busiest railway stations in the country. Hundreds, thousands of people rushed past his doorway every day, twice a day. Rushed *past*, not in. After a while he found he was out of money, so he put out closing down sale notices.

Hundreds and thousands of people rushed **into** his shop and now he is very wealthy and busy running discount pharmacies in high traffic areas. He had accidently found a hole in the market.

Similarly restaurants tend to congregate in the same street so that they can catch the hungry en masse. On every street block or shopping centre there is a set of businesses similar to those nearby. Why? Because people do what is easy—they shop where they can park their car and do it all at once. They travel down the same tracks for their needs, time after time after time.

Germain Marquis agrees. He said when he had his restaurant, Le Marquis, in Sandton, Johannesburg, all his clientele came from Sandton. When he moved a few kilometres to Morningside, he was busy, but it was with Morningside locals.

Then he moved back to Sandton and opened the Sausalito. Suddenly all the old crowd was back. When he asked why they had not come a couple of kilometres down the road to Morningside, they all said it was too far!

In Australia, Thomas Cook had a busy office at the north end of Bankstown shopping centre. One day I analysed the postcodes of their clients and found they all came from the north—they drove into the shopping centre from that point, shopped at that end of the shopping centre and drove away.

If Thomas Cook had put in offices on the south, east and west sides they would have quadrupled their business.

The Mars Bar people found the same thing in New York. The city blocks are big enough to have multiple corner stores, and analysis showed that different outlets sold different sweets, depending on the socio-economic standing of the people coming the quickest way down their "tracks" for their supplies.

When you choose the business you want to be in, let it be a simple one to promote—regularly and relentlessly—within 90 days. People are complex and simple at the same time. The least amount of effort required, mentally and physically, to make the decision of a purchase, the more successful you will be.

> *"If you have a job without aggravations, you don't have a job."* Malcolm Forbes

Allow yourself to become as single-minded about your business as the Coca-Cola Company. Coca-Cola has spent billions on marketing and continues to do so, to reach an average of about ten to twenty per cent of the world soft drink market.

This giant, international company consistently spends a colossal amount ($500 million in the United States alone) to sell its product, single-mindedly saying the same things over and over again, in what look like new and different ways.

Single-minded repetition

The reason it's necessary to be single-minded is that only about one per cent of the human brain is available to take in any corporate message. Our own lives tie up about ninety-nine per cent of our brains: work, home, finances, children, in-laws, weddings, divorces, medical issues, birthdays and holidays.

With all of that and more on our mind, why would we be listening to the incredible volume of advertising messages that assault our eyes and ears every day? Who cares, when the rest of the day is falling down around our feet or shrilling down our ears?

Regular, single-minded contact with prospects is the only way to make them take notice of you. You may have found that your first round of mailing and phoning netted a one-half to one per cent response, with people actually saying "Yes" to appointments and some even giving you business.

This suggests that your mailing package and phoning program were successful, so do not change anything significantly.

With the second round, there is the temptation to design something entirely new in order to excite yourself and everybody around you. Resist that temptation. You can design a variation on your original theme, but at all costs defend your right to bore yourself and your workplace associates.

Some examples: the Christian Dior pink oval stands out on packs you have no idea about except that they are from Dior; the Mercedes star would say Mercedes no matter where you found it; roses will always stand for love and romance; diamonds have little more glitter than glass but the endless romantic advertising ensures that no wise man would ever give a piece of glass instead.

Yes, you can repeat yourself endlessly, as Coca-Cola does. When you think of straying from the path, ask yourself, "Has Coca-Cola ever changed its image significantly?"

It has always been a fun product for lively beautiful people who go leaping around beaches and mountains and cities, in and out of surf and snow, up and down and around on rollerblades and who do wonderful, happy things while drinking Coke. If Coca-Cola's message hasn't changed significantly over the years, your own successful message need not change either. Continue to bore yourself; you won't be a bore to the outside world.

You can vary your theme, as in Coke/Coca-Cola or Big Mac/

McDonald's, providing you create a relevant sound, but don't deviate too much, to the Big Cold One or the Big Hot One, for example.

It is too long a phrase to be catchy, unlike Coke or Big Mac. Big Chill and Big Hot don't work either, because they have emotional overtones of freezing and boiling—an unpleasant way to be drinking and eating. Always avoid anything unpleasant!

If it's trite and boring, do it!

> *"If you want a place in the sun, prepare to put up with a few blisters."* Abigail Van Buren

Your message may seem trite and boring to you because you are so close to your product. However, the rest of the world doesn't know about your great product story. When you have a clear idea of who you are, what your product is and what it has to offer, don't give up. Keep on offering it until your prospects notice it, too.

The first time you put your product message in a covering letter, say something like, "May we introduce you to ...?" The second time around, you can say, "May we remind you that ...?" The third time you could say, "Again, may we call your attention to ...?" The fourth time around try, "We would like to remind you ..."

Never give up on your basic, central message. You are exactly who you are. Present your product or service continually and without much deviation. If you deviate, you may confuse that tiny bit of the one per cent that is listening to your message and you will be the loser.

Make it easy for people to find you. Have your address and contact number big and bold. Pass your letterhead through your fax machine and make sure the numbers are still clear to read.

Of all the faxes I get, about 10% are readable in that area, as corporate ID designers still think people mail letters when we know that we fax far faster and more effectively.

So stay with it. When you are yawning at the mere thought of ever saying the same thing again, when you are bored to tears with those words or pictures, that's when the outside world is beginning to listen to you.

To a travel client we recommended selling Bali holidays on a "Buy-one-get-one-free" basis. The travel agency groaned. They were sick to death of the sound of Bali. But all available travel statistics showed that the youth market was still very interested in travelling to Bali and was not in the slightest bit bored by the sound or sights of Bali.

"Go with the flow," we said. "You want to get young people inside the door, so capture them by offering what they want. When it is trite and boring to you, do it!" It worked. The travel company established a good base of young travellers and went on to sell them many other products in the youth holiday range.

Remember, repeat yourself until you are so sick with boredom that you wish your product or service had never been invented. Stay in touch with prospects in a positive and caring way, within the three-month cycle. Your only mission in your business life is to help people clearly understand what it is you offer so that they will buy from you in their own time.

Make being trite and boring work for you (yawn, sob!)

> *"Some people say three is the magic number and others say it's seven. But I'm here to tell you, Oliver, the only magic number is one."* Fagin to Oliver Twist

Have you repeated your central message to the point of being bored to tears in the past? Have you briefed your advertising agency to come back to you time and again with the same central message? Or did you cry out for something new and exciting and even move on to another agency to get a bright and vibrant new look?

If you did you are not the only one. In America alone, around eighty per cent of all clients move from one advertising agency to another within five years, probably for this very reason. It takes about two years to get a new advertising agency settled into the culture of the company they are trying to work with and yet the first cracks of the honeymoon period are evident within eighteen months. Another move is imminent.

It is no wonder that the public ignores so much of what is thrown at it. The ads are being prepared by people who know in their heart of hearts that no matter what they do, the next advertising manager in the job will call for five or six or even forty agencies to come up with something bright and new, the account will move and they will be out of a job—again.

I had an advertising manager from a major company tell me that the first thing he does is move the business to show who is in charge. But not for long. Given a few months or years he himself will move on for whatever reason and it will all start again.

Defend your right to be boring, but boring only to yourself. Get out everything that the public sees from your company and lay this enormous bundle on the boardroom table. Look for that central message, style, colour, layout, theme, feeling.

Look for anything that makes you think the outside world has a chance of recognising your product message, be it on radio, TV, buses, billboards, newspapers, magazines or even matchbox covers!

Look for that continuity in your letters, brochures, flyers, instruction manuals. If you see a boring sameness, congratulations! If you do not, don't change your agency, just work with them to make it happen.

In addition to your ninety-day (or less) contacts with prospects, there is no harm in creating positive publicity about your product or service. A good story in your local print or electronic media can do wonders for your business.

What is involved in writing press releases and getting them published?

Getting your story into the media

> *"Glory is fleeting, but obscurity is forever."*
> Napoleon Bonaparte (1769–1821)

Have you ever tried to get into a restaurant the day after it's been well reviewed in the local newspaper? Such is the power of free publicity, the lines can reach around the block. In addition to increasing visibility in your community, press coverage can be copied and used as part of your mailing package to prospective clients. When you are written up in a magazine that is printed in four colours, get the front cover reprinted as well as the piece inside that is about you. The promotional effect is enormous, compared to a dull black and white reprint. In that way the article about you becomes a permanent part of your promotional material and can be seen by people who missed it when it appeared in the media.

You can generate such good publicity by taking the following steps:

1. Read through your local newspaper. Look at the length (number of words) of its articles and what subjects are seen to be of interest to its readers. If you live in a major metropolitan area, don't limit yourself to the largest newspaper or the major radio or television stations. Study local suburban papers and smaller radio stations to determine if they are the right place for your news release.
2. Decide whether you respond more positively to printed articles when they are accompanied by a photo and, if so, plan to include a photo with the piece you hope to get published.
3. Check the newspaper or magazine's address and staff listing for the person most likely to deal with an article about your business. Call up to confirm. If the person is not right, make sure you get the correct name and title before hanging up. If there is a gatekeeper, be sure to get that name too.
4. Phone when your piece is ready, explain what your press release is about and ask what time it would be convenient to bring it in. Even if they cannot see you in person to receive your material, you will have alerted them to look for it.
5. Turn up at the newspaper office at the right time with a beautifully prepared press release and an 8" x 10" black-and-white glossy photo to support the story. Introduce yourself to the person whose name you have and ask whether this person feels your article could be used. Or could they perhaps advise you how to improve it?
6. Maintain contact, keep trying, turn up in person. Always hone your skills. Continue to read all relevant magazines, newspapers and trade journals for their style. Adapt yourself to their ways; clip articles that you think you could write, even about some business unlike your own; and practise, practise, practise.

A tourist was lost in New York and stopped a couple hurrying by. "How do I get to Carnegie Hall?" he demanded. "Practise, practise, practise," came the reply.

What is a press/news release?

> *"There are only two ways of telling the complete truth—anonymously and posthumously."* Thomas Sowell

A press or news release is a short, snappy piece sent to all forms of print and electronic media in the hope that it will be published free of cost and bring your business or product to the attention of potential users.

All print media use articles (see "Articles" section below) based on press releases, to fill in space not taken up by paid advertising. Such articles are written by in-house or freelance writers and by organised business people who know how to get press releases expanded into articles.

If you are newsworthy, and there's time on a particular news day, you'll get a mention on the radio, or the TV station may send a camera team to cover your event.

As an example of the power of the press, an earlier edition of this book was selling quite well in South Africa and reviews had appeared in the press. I had also been on radio several times. Then I was on TV for two minutes. That week the book sold out across South Africa, and the TV station reported back that they had calls for weeks afterwards to verify the title of the book and the name of the author.

They themselves were delighted with the response as it showed that people were watching the show (Good Morning South Africa) across the nation and remembering the content long after the show had moved on. If there is a TV talk show, do everything you can to appear on it! Remember, you get what you focus on.

> *"The trouble with life in the fast lane is that you get to the other end in an awful hurry."* John Jensen

Practise the five Ws of a press release from this example

Who: Your business.
What: Is having a special sale offering up to eighty per cent off selected merchandise (or is giving a free blouse with every dress bought, or a blouse and skirt ensemble for half price, etc.).
When: During the first week of December, with extended hours from 8 a.m. to 10 p.m.
Where: Your address.
Why: To introduce the community to your new antique-look Asian silks.

Cut out an interesting short piece about a business from your local newspaper and see if you can match up the contents to the five Ws above. Next step is to practise for yourself.

With your outline in hand, you can write your news release easily by following all five points as you progress. Be sure to include your full name, business name, address and phone number, so you can be contacted if additional information is needed. Make it as easy as possible for the editor of the magazine, newspaper, radio or TV station to reach you.

The 8 x 10 glossy black-and-white photograph

If you are going to submit a photo with your news release, you can get a good professional photographer to take it for you, or you can put a roll of black-and-white film in your camera and do it yourself. Photograph only the images that support your news release and take many shots to ensure at least one good photo will result.

Try to adjust your major points of interest so they will appear everywhere except in the centre of the photo. Have the major points of interest about one-third in from the edges, being approximately on the Golden Line (see the section on colour and design for more on that subject).

Have small prints made and examine them for good impact, clarity, interest and relevance. Then the best of them should be blown up to an 8" x 10" glossy. Get several copies made if you are sending your release to more than one news organisation.

On the back of the photograph, place a label containing words that could be used as a caption for the photo. Thus, if your story and picture get separated at the newspaper office, they can be matched up again.

Do not write on the back of the photo; tape your message on

instead. Type out your statement neatly on an adhesive-backed label or along the width of a sheet of white paper that is nearly the size of your photo. Cut it out with a small margin top and bottom and paste or tape it on. Never spoil your photograph by writing on the back.

Typing your news release professionally

Use blank typing paper, head it "News Release" and date it. Keep wide margins, double spacing, and two double line spaces between paragraphs. Keep the press release to one page if you possibly can.

If not, make the reader turn to the next page by ending the first page in mid-sentence (but not mid-word). Be sure to include full details of your name, address, phone and fax numbers on every sheet so the editor of the paper/magazine/radio/TV station can contact you easily.

Use everything you have learned about promoting new business to keep in touch, regularly, relentlessly and caringly. Say thank you as you go. You will be pleased by the attention you are likely to get if your releases are thoughtful, correct and relevant to the readers and viewers of your local media.

You may feel encouraged enough to write longer pieces, e.g. articles of around one thousand words on items of local interest. Again, be sure to do your research well as to the kind of articles accepted by the various forms of media.

What is an article?

An article is usually longer than a press release—say, one thousand words or longer—and allows for a fuller development of the subject.

An article about a local merchant, for instance, would not cover a particular sale as in the previous press release example. Instead, it would be a researched piece on the entrepreneur's early beginnings in a small family business, the success and growth of her businesses around the world, followed by her decision to leave the running of her empire to her nieces while she researched natural silk dyes in Asia. The article would end by revealing that her intent now is to bring the colours and feel of antique silk to today's easy, relaxed fashions.

Make good PR happen for you

> *"As scarce as truth is, the supply has always been in excess of the demand."* Josh Billings (1818–1885)

Become addicted to the media that serves your immediate business catchment area. Analyse where your best clients come from, then ask them what newspapers, magazines and trade journals they read.

Also what radio and TV stations they like. When you visit their offices, check their tables for the journals they subscribe to and ask if you can borrow some.

Then read, read, read until you understand the style of writing that these newsprint media use and like. Listen to the radio stations for their kind of special sound. Is it noisy, brash, urgent—or soft, gentle, undemanding? Or something more businesslike in between. Similarly, what type of program does their preferred TV channel specialise in?

Practise, practise, practise those styles. And do pay attention to details. For instance, check the type of photograph they are interested in, such as action/people/scenery/product.

Practise, practise, practise until you get it right and get free publicity because of it, in just the media you should be in. I heard of one businessman who regularly gets free publicity in his church magazine and good business results from that exposure.

Key points to remember

Be absolutely consistent in your follow-up messages—to the point of being bored to sobs yourself. When you feel you can take no more, have a drink of Coke and remember how consistent Coca-Cola is in portraying their message. Coke after Coke after Coke. Let it be the same for you, same for you, same for you.

Why pay for press advertising when you can get it for free? The Body Shop for instance has never paid for an advertisement since the day they started. Learn the art of writing press releases and articles.

Take a course in photography (black-and-white and colour). Read all the trade journals, newspapers and magazines that your clients/customers read. Listen to their radio stations. Watch their TV stations.

Understand how they see, hear and feel regarding any business issues on which you can have an impact. Then practise writing in the styles of their reading, listening and viewing. When you are comfortable in your communication, the chances are that your PR release or article will be picked up.

Has it ever happened to you that just when prospects were about to buy, they wandered off, murmuring something about coming back later? We can never really know what goes on inside their heads, but if you find the reason why they are interested in the product, you can make a relevant special offer which may close the deal.

Step Nine

Maintain a competitive edge

> *"Every time a friend succeeds, I die a little."* Gore Vidal

Promoting the sale

You have provided dynamic written materials, you have had a successful appointment, the potential client seems pleased by what you have to offer. Still, he or she is wavering about giving you the business project and as always, you realise that you have hungry competitors wanting the business, too. In this case, a special offer on your part can make the difference. It says, "I really want your business."

The essence of sales promotion is that it must be easily understood by the public and relevant to your product. It will seem ludicrous to consumers to get a free embroidery kit if they are buying a puppy! With this principle in mind, let's look at some industry examples.

Promotional techniques

In hairdressing, you can promote your business using hairdressing products. In fashion, you can promote using accessories or perfumes. With books you can offer membership in a book club.

Your offer always has to sound right and be related in some way to your product or service. Here are a few types of special offers you can consider; they represent some of the best promotional vehicles I've seen in the past few years—with the exception of competitions, which I have included for discussion only.

A free gift with purchase is probably the most successful sales promotion on earth. A high-quality gift lives on in the memory as a favourable experience of dealing with your company. My client Thomas Cook, as a free gift with purchase, gave away a beautiful leather travel wallet with separate pockets for all the items travellers need to carry.

Made of the finest leather and very well constructed, these wallets look good ten years later and are an ongoing quality testimonial for Thomas Cook. I still use mine and am delighted every time I line up at the check-in counter to have such a useful and attractive item. The offer also brought the company a great amount of business at the time.

If you really want to move your product, think of offering a free gift with the purchase of a certain dollar amount of merchandise or services: a free sunroof when you buy a car; free shirts or ties with a suit; free software with a computer; an extra month's free advertising space with a six-month campaign; free shampoo and conditioner with a hair colour treatment.

Buy one, get one free. Buy one suit or dress and you will receive another free. Have your eyes examined and another family member's examination is free. This is also a very powerful promotional technique which gives the customer two for the price of one, or fifty per cent off. Of the three possible ways of expressing this offer, the "buy-one-get-one-free" statement is stronger than "two for the price of one" or "fifty per cent off". The first phrase contains the word "free", which is one of the most powerful words in the English language.

Buy two (or more) and get one free is also powerful, depending on the price of the purchased item. For instance, buy eight motor cars and get one free would be a great offer to a company buying a fleet and it would be more impressively conveyed than would be: "twelve per cent off the price of each of the eight cars".

The Peninsula Hotel in Hong Kong buys Rolls-Royce cars in large numbers and I have often wondered what sort of an offer Rolls-Royce makes.

Do they get one car free when they buy eight, I wonder? The only trouble with Rolls-Royce cars is that the luggage carrying capacity is small and when major players in the clothes stakes came to town, such as Imelda Marcos, we had to send out several trucks for the luggage.

A banded offer involves putting two things together with a band around them. When you sell four litres of paint banded with a half-litre of turpentine, make the banded price somewhat less than the price of both if sold separately.

You have now created a promotion worthy of attention and you will sell more of each item than ever before. A toothbrush with toothpaste or mouthwash is a good banded offer; so is pantihose with a second pair, detergent with fabric softener and deodorant with talcum powder. These kinds of offers work very well.

Price reductions will get customers flocking in, but use such sales discreetly, so that you have no more than two per year. You don't want to appear to be buying your way out of trouble. When you have this type of sale, make it such a terrific value that people line up for your product. Those who buy merchandise at your sales once or twice and are treated well may develop loyalty to your business and come back again outside of the sales season.

It seems that the stores with the best sales also allow you to return the sales goods for a full refund. Clients will say, "And they even gave me all my money back, without any argument." The less significant companies usually have a no-returns policy. Which would you shop at in the future?

Sampling is also a popular sales promotion technique, where a small sample of the product is delivered to your home. Many years ago a new soap powder appeared in my letterbox, and when used, refused to dissolve in any temperature of water. It just swirled around in little pellets with the washing. Apart from arousing my wrath, the sample achieved nothing accept my refusal to ever buy the product. However, if the product is a good one, it can encourage purchase when the first use has proven its worth.

Vouchers and coupons arrive in your home as inserts in newspapers or magazines or in household letterbox drops. They offer you money off the company's product to encourage purchase and trial use. After that it is over to the shopper to decide whether the item is bought again.

Quality service can be the best sales promotion technique!

You can do simple things, such as taking care of people's parcels as a kind gesture and security measure. In New York you have to hand in any bag bigger than a small handbag, and even though it is an anti-theft process, it allows you to shop hands-free.

Recently in a well-respected department store, I tried to check in my overnight bag and was advised quite firmly that it was against security regulations. I could not carry it and shop at the same time, so I left. In this case they even made it seem a federal offence for me to have asked! I just do not feel like going back, despite having shopped there for many years.

Collector's items can work well too. KLM Royal Dutch Airlines ran an excellent promotion offering everybody who flew first class, a porcelain miniature of a Dutch house filled with liqueur. People bought first-class tickets as never before so they could display these collectibles on their desks and show that they were high-class travellers of the world. If the collectible item you have in mind has a "certain something", go for it, but test its appeal beforehand.

In fact, test every promotional offer of any kind before going all the way. You can save yourself a lot of time and money if you test first and then finetune it if it seems to be working. "Doing something small in the corner first" is a very good technique for instituting any form of change. If you impose a major change on an organisation, it usually fails from fear, ignorance and confusion. If you do a test and it works well, the whole organisation hears of it and wants it.

The personality presenter: someone with name recognition endorses your product. However, celebrity endorsements have pitfalls. The endorser has to be totally believable, or the whole promotion becomes memorable for its failure. So in general, avoid paying some powerful "name" to endorse your product unless it is the equivalent of Florence Nightingale for bandages, Arnold Schwarzenegger for a fitness campaign, or Ernie Nels for golf!

> *"Anyone can win, unless there happens to be a second entry."* George Ade, 1866–1944

Competitions. In any competition, there must be some element of skill, such as writing a poem about why you would like to fly British Airways to London, with the winner getting a return trip for two.

There are complex state laws governing competitions. Moreover, competitions are not as successful as other techniques in promoting sales because people never really believe they are going to win.

For the time and effort involved in putting together prizes for a competition, it would be much better to make a "free gift with purchase" offer or a "buy-one-get-one-free" offer. In many instances a retailer can get free gifts from the suppliers of the product so the end result is perhaps no more expensive than the competition process, but far more effective.

Remember, when you are working to close the sale with a prospect, consider promotional offers and how you can adjust some of these to suit your particular situation. If you are in the service industry, try giving a discount when the account is paid within five working days.

This can work so well that you may find you have fewer bad debts. One of my clients paid an art studio within five days in order to get a five per cent reduction, while letting all other companies not offering a discount wait ninety to one hundred and twenty days.

In Singapore a hotel decided to offer a flat rate but got so many complaints from local companies that they marked the room rates up again and then gave the expected fifteen per cent deduction to corporate clients. The end result was exactly the same, but saved "face".

Similarly, if you are in the consulting industry and do not wish to discount your fees, simply charge more and then offer a discount if paid in a period of time that suits you, such as five working days. If the bill is not paid within that time, you are owed the extra.

If yours is a product, probe for the prospect's needs and make your offer accordingly, such as free lawn mowing for a year if they hire you to landscape their garden, a garden umbrella if they buy a particular type of garden furniture, an extra twelve bottles of wine with the purchase of ten cases.

I met a man in a car showroom who told me he had bought his previous car because they were giving away a free milkshake machine. He had two children so thought it a good idea.

I have seen a suburb at standstill because the local council was giving away free trees and I even saw an area in total chaos because the local greengrocer was selling two cabbages for the price of one.

You need not go that far. Instead you may wish to use a standard gift such as charity chocolates or peppermints. You could buy them outright and then offer them to your clients and customers as they leave. This little gift works just as well in a professional services organisation as it does at retail level. People are people—they get tired and dry and a "good cause" peppermint or tasty piece of chocolate is a great pick-me-up.

Managing your promotions

The reality of good promotional activities is that they take time. You can't just leap out of bed and decide to have an eighty-per-cent-off sale when you get to work that day.

Planning four to six months in advance is about right. That way you can do a little each day and have your Mother's Day promotion, for instance, happen comfortably, with time to spare to fix up the bits you may forget, such as the window notices or the envelopes to be ordered, or the mailing to your best customers for a preview day. If you do a little each day, it does not break up your normal working day too much and adds another interest to your life.

Why not use the Saatchi & Saatchi three-month cycle for promotional activities? You could plan to have four similar promotions to your client and prospect base each year. Your planning processes would become almost repetitive and therefore much easier to do.

Remember the principle of saying and doing the same things, all the time, so that the public finally gets to notice you? For instance, in the service industry you could have four open days a year, or four half-day workshops with leading gods of industry. As a retailer you could have four "free-gift-with-purchase" promotions; or four "extra-product-free" weeks.

Planning several promotions over a year means making up a calendar of all the actions that have to be done in chronological order and sticking to it. If you are a retailer, for instance, wanting to promote Valentine's Day, Easter, Mother's Day, Father's Day, Christmas and New Year, you should be thinking and acting on those activities every day of your working life.

The skill is to find a simple, effective promotion that works for you and will only need tweaking to adapt it to all occasions. This is a great timesaver and it has the advantage of bringing a consistent look and sound to your advertising, point of sale and direct marketing communications.

Make sales promotion techniques work for you

> *"Veni, vidi, Visa (We came, we saw, we went shopping)."*
> Jan Barrett

Buy some women's magazines and notice all the sales promotion activities within their covers. Try to understand why the advertisers would make these offers; read all the fine print to see just how complex an operation a competition can be, for instance. When you plan to do sales promotion, remember these key issues:

Keep it relevant to the objectives, to the product and to the needs of the customer/client or prospect.

Keep it simple. No-one ever went broke underestimating the amount of time available to the consumer or client. We are all too busy to work our way through complicated offers—and your competitor may be offering a simple alternative. Winning a sale can be as easy as keeping it simple.

Keep it quality. Do nothing cheap; do everything well. The good and the bad live on forever after the promotion. If you give shoddy goods you will be shunned; if you give quality goods you will establish an immediate rapport of respect between you and the client/prospect.

We look now at using special offers in contract negotiations to build an ongoing successful relationship with your new client.

The contract is still to be signed

> *"Life is what happens while you are busy making other plans."* John Lennon (1940–1980)

Why a contract? Because you want to get paid! There is no point in getting into a relationship where money is involved and then finding you have done all the work for no money or no proof that the money was owed. This is especially important if you work as an agent and there is commission owed—which could be conveniently forgotten if you don't get it down on paper.

While the prospect has identified a need for your product or service and you have made a relevant special offer, you may still find yourself without a signed contract.

Perhaps you thought that you and your prospect had come to an agreement about a contract, only to find that your prospect's thoughts were not in alignment with yours. There's always that moment when you return from a meeting thinking that it's all falling into place, but then, something often happens that is called "post-purchase dissonance": everything seems to fall apart and you're completely unprepared for it.

Here are some issues to watch out for during your negotiations with a prospect:

1. Always remember that people buy from greed, fear and laziness. Did you touch some or all of those buttons?
2. Be aware that there's often more to come after you've reached a verbal agreement with a potential client. A verbal agreement is usually a general understanding; a written contract requires attention to detail and considerable compromise to get everything down and agreed to in black and white.
3. Get into the habit of agreeing on the little things before tackling the big ones. Strive for good and fair solutions.
4. Be considerate and flexible with the client or customer, remembering that contracts are not a legal document until signed. You don't want to scare people away by behaving as if your contract is iron-clad when in fact you are willing to make concessions. Perhaps the prospect has already conceded something elsewhere, or it's an unusually large order, or the profits resulting from the contract will be very high. Be thoughtful of the client and your future. Do not kill the golden goose.
5. Let the client know that you intend the negotiations to be friendly and to result in a contract that both parties are happy to be entering. One of the problems with contracts is that people tend to consider the draft wording to be carved in stone. Not so; every word can be changed up to and including signing, providing both parties agree with the changes. But don't make changes just for the power of doing so.
6. Describe your pricing so that it's easily understood: this is what it costs and why. Avoid subclauses and penalty clauses that make clients feel they are being punished if they do something the slightest bit different.

7. Check that your contract is relevant and readable. Don't rehash an old contract. Make sure it sounds as if it were written especially for this particular client. In addition, your contract will be easier to sign if its language is plain English. When a muddled contract document itself becomes an issue, you're likely to find yourself facing costly delays in getting started.
8. Consider putting a clause into the contract that offers a discount on the cost of your product or service or a significant and relevant free gift if the agreement is signed by a certain date. When the offer is worthwhile, this can work wonders in getting the agreement through the various levels of approval.
9. Be aware that the only good negotiation is one in which both sides believe they have won a little. Think how great you feel when you come away from a discussion that led to what you wanted. It's even better when both sides feel that way.
10. Recognise that the contract you sign today may need to be altered in the future because your needs, or the client's needs, may change. How you react to a client's changed circumstances will impact on future contracts with the company and on referrals. Maintain a long-term view, be flexible and be sure that the new negotiations benefit both sides.

When a closing is not a closing

> *"It is better to be a mouse in a cat's mouth than a man in a lawyer's hands."* Spanish proverb

The point made in the preceding paragraph is so important that I will reiterate it: closing the sale is often not closing the sale at all, it's just the beginning of many such interactions. Of course, once a contract is signed, you can foolishly demand that clients stick to the letter of the agreement, in spite of their changed needs. However, if you insist on taking such an inflexible position, you might get through the term of that one contract (or fight it out in the courts) but there are not likely to be further contracts.

That kind of an attitude doesn't add up to long-term business. Be adaptable; you want to win for today and you also want to win for tomorrow. Try not to win the battle but lose the war. Rather let both you and the client win, for future peace and prosperity.

Be fair and friendly in your contract negotiations

> *"Honesty is the best image."* Ziggy (Tom Wilson)

Back to the files for some contracts. Get out any that you have been required to sign. Now ask yourself these questions:
Did I understand exactly what I was getting into?
Did I feel closer to the other person because of the signing of the contract?
Was it laid out in an easy-to-read, plain English style?
Was the tone warm and friendly?
Would I look forward to another contract negotiation with this person/company?
Did I feel fairly and intelligently treated?
Was the layout of the contract well done, the quality of the paper good, the overall feeling one of importance, respect and dignity?

Now get out some contracts that you and/or your lawyers have drawn up for clients and customers to sign. Stand in the shoes of the client and ask the same questions as above. If you are not delighted with the answers, see if you can reword and redesign future contracts to change some of the not-so-good elements.

> *"Lawyers, I suppose, were children once."*
> Charles Lamb, 1775–1834

Key points to remember

Make relevant special offers to bring forward the purchase decision in your favour. "Free gift with purchase" is probably the strongest, with "buy one get one free" a close second.

When you get to the contract stage, draft a communication that totally focuses on the client from their point of view. Stress that every word is changeable until a mutually satisfactory agreement is reached.

Use this stage to establish good working relationships. Start off in the spirit of harmony that will become the springboard for all future negotiations.

Step Ten

How to keep yourself organised

> *"I never travel without my diary. One should always have something sensational to read."* Oscar Wilde (1854–1900)

Time management

> *"Doing the right thing seems to be more important than doing things right."* Peter Drucker

Get rid of the unimportant things first so that they never become important, do the urgent and important things next and then let the other things interrupt—this is the dream I have for my day. Up to the "urgent" point I seem to be in control, but after that I am all too often overidden by other people's needs. So how can I (and we) change the effect that "urgent" has on us?

First of all we need to know what our objectives are—not only every day for the day, but also for the week, the month, the year and beyond. Be effective and efficient, but effective first and foremost. Our business and promotional plans, our strategic purpose are what give us control over other people's interruptive techniques.

We have all experienced the telephone call that comes at the critical moment of a discussion; the staff member who urgently needs our help to finish a job not attended to until too late; the manager or associate who walks in the door and demands a meeting, now.

What do we do? Too often we respond, react and overreact to these pressures from people and things. We answer the phone, help the laziest member of the team and go off to the meeting unprepared and unwilling. There goes the day, blown as usual.

If, however, our working days were measured by the agreed business and promotional objectives that we had jointly set and which we reviewed and revised constantly, how might we have managed instead?

The phone could have been put on hold (either through an answering machine or a staff member). A specific time could have been allocated to help and review the performance of that lazy staff member. A rational explanation could have been given re the meeting: the job you were working on was urgent and important but you would be free after 4.30 p.m.

All these power responses are relative to the objectives that were commonly agreed as being important for that day, that week, or longer. You take control by choosing time scales within which you can operate effectively and efficiently. Consider taking specific periods of time for the important issues. Try sixty minutes of privacy for yourself, then open up for messages and be available for the next thirty minutes to respond to staff and management needs and return phone calls. Then close down for another sixty minutes, reopen for thirty.

I suggest trying a sixty-minute cycle to begin with, because that is the recommended changeover time for driving long distances. Have you tried driving that way? If so, did you look forward to the changeover both ways? Perhaps you found at first you wanted to rest and watch the scenery and next you wanted to drive and get on with it. Similarly, you might enjoy shutting down for an hour of private time, knowing that you are going to have a cup of coffee and get in touch with the world again shortly.

Alternatively, I met an executive who now takes and returns phone calls only between 3 p.m. and 5.30 p.m. After only three weeks of this regime, almost everyone now calls him between those hours. They had learned two things: one, that he was not available until that time and two, that he always returned calls on the day, as promised. No hassles, no problems; people simply adapted to what they saw as a very fair, effective and efficient process.

The answer to time management, I suggest, is to know what your objectives are and stick to achieving them. Ensure that the balance is in your favour by allocating only as much time as you can truly spare to the interruptions and plagues of the day. Use a tickler box (divided into month, week, days) to remind you of the follow-up calls that you promised to make—and will be remembered forever for so doing! And delegate, delegate, delegate.

> *"Never put off until tomorrow what you can do the day after tomorrow."* Mark Twain, 1835–1910

Managing meetings

> *"The goal of inanimate objects is to resist man and ultimately defeat him."* Russell Baker

All too often meetings end up going round and round the same subjects, everyone putting in their bit, little being resolved. Simon & Schuster in America required that no problem was to come to a meeting unless the following analysis had been written up and distributed beforehand:

1. What is the problem? ....

   ....

2. What caused the problem? ....

   ....

3. Three/four solutions for solving the problem are:

   a. ....

   b. ....

   c. ....

   d. ....

4. Of these possible solutions I recommend .... for the following reasons:

   ....

   ....

   ....

Often the problem never gets to the meeting, because the person owning the problem solves it by doing this work first. Here is an evaluation for use after meetings to find out how you can improve the next one.

Why was the meeting called?

....

Was the meeting really necessary?

....

Was the purpose of the meeting met?

....

Was the time convenient and the place suitable?

....

Was the time limit met, and was it realistic to begin with?

....

Did the agenda need to be sent out in advance? If so, was it?

....

Should all participants have had input into the agenda? If so, did they?

....

Were supporting documents needed? If so, were they distributed?

....

Did participants read and study them prior to the meeting, if asked to do so?

....

Did the discussions remain relevant through self-management or through constant reminder?

....

Did the participants stay with the agenda?

....

Did all relevant people participate in the discussions?

....

Were accurate records kept and effective minutes distributed within forty-eight hours?

....

Are follow-up issues likely to be attended to? Or ignored until pursued?

....

In the opinion of the group, was everyone there that needed to be?

....

Again, in the opinion of the group, was anyone there that should not have been?

....

How satisfied was the group with the meeting?

....

According to those who attended, what changes should be made?

....

If you had controlled this meeting, how would you do it better next time?

....

How happy are you with the follow-up?

....

Recently I took a group of sales executives through this process and we realised two things:

First, that they had underestimated the importance of the Japanese process of involving all levels of the decision makers and influencers, from top to bottom, centre left to centre right—"figure eight".

And second, that their follow-up left something to be desired because they feared the answer "no". They also lacked a closing technique because their product (in-house catering) was not urgent. So long as their people were eating, changing to a better, more healthy and cost-efficient process was not important.

We workshopped the problem using the philosophy that people buy from greed, fear and laziness. What offer could they make that would bring forward the purchase decision?

We decided that a fixed management fee for eighteen months (if the decision was made in the next two months) would be a strong motivator. Snap! the deal was done.

Using the meeting analysis form can open up a whole new way of thinking. Try it!

It is important to remember that all meetings go through the following phases—child, adolescent, adult, old age. At first, people are nervous and irritable, thinking things like, "Why am I here? Why can't they simply write a memo and let me get on with my work?"

Then the adolescent phase kicks in: they drop their papers, fight for where they are going to sit, jostle for the tea and the biscuits, tell this week's funny stories.

At the adult stage, they decide that if they buckle down and get on with it, they may get out in time to sign the mail and go home.

Then old age kicks in: members get tired and crotchety and won't "play" any longer. The key issue is to listen to their language during the adult phase and never to respond to their old-age comments.

In the adult phase they will express interest, ask for more information, make positive remarks.

In the old-age phase, they will say things like "We will call you when we are ready to proceed"; "We will let you know when the budgets come through"; "Don't call us, we will call you". This you ignore. Simply remember the positive words in the adult phase and respond accordingly.

In America I met a woman who did not have meetings, she had "deli-days". She copied the process used by busy food counters: take a number and wait to be called. On her deli-days, staff took a number and waited for their turn to discuss their problems and issues with her. Keen staff got in early to get the earliest numbers. Each person was given as much time as they needed.

Colour-code "Important and Urgent"; "Important, not Urgent"; "Not Important, Can Appear Urgent"; "Not Important, Not Urgent".

Stephen Covey, the author of *The 7 Habits of Highly Effective People* (which is on the recommended reading list at the back of this book), has a matrix on time management issues. His four quadrants are as follows:

1. *Important and urgent:* crises, pressing problems, deadline-driven projects. Consider having a large red file for this.

2. *Important, not urgent:* preparation, *new-business activities, crisis prevention, values clarification, planning, relationship-building, true recreation. Consider having a large blue file for this.
3. *Not important but can appear urgent:* interruptions, some calls, mail, some reports, some meetings, many current pressing matters, many popular activities. These could be in a green file.
4. *Not important, not urgent:* trivia, busy work, some mail, some phone calls, time-wasters, many pleasant activities. These could be in a yellow file.

To repeat myself: unfortunately number two, the "important, not urgent" area, is often the one that gets the least attention. New-business activities fall in this area all too often. People mean to get on with it, but somehow they are too busy.

Preparation time for meetings is too often done in the car or the plane. And who has time to prepare properly for a business plan, a strategic purpose for the future?—let alone revise it constantly in view of the changing nature of the world. Yet planning is the key to the future, and the objectives within the plan are the control factor in our time management processes.

In the last fifteen or so years of listening to and researching company issues, I have found that the worldwide problem is lack of planning—or if planning is done, the implementing of those plans. And worse still, if planning is done, there is little if any involvement at the coalface level.

A recent client, the second largest in the world in their field, explained how the planning was done for their sales team. The product managers went away and did it together, then told the sales team what they were to do.

The sad part is of course that the product managers don't get out and sell, so how can they possibly know what it is like out there? And consequently the sales people had no respect for their "plans".

Crisis prevention, rather than putting out fires, takes planning time too. So often we hope that things will go away like the

* Though I believe that new-business activities should be in Important and Urgent. The reason why people do not get on with new-business contacting is that they always think they will catch up tomorrow. If you put it under Important and Urgent, then it is today's priority.

recession: things like confused and disorganised government regulations, staff resignations, out-of-control costs, gradual disappearance of the traditional marketplace. Even acknowledging these issues is hard, without having to find the time—and the solutions—to fix them.

Values clarification can mean hours or days meditating on that one subject: what are the corporate and personal values you bring to your staff and your clients or customers? How do you express these values, instill them, maintain them? Are you being true to yourself, or paying lip service to the flavour of the month?

Relationship-building is what the business and personal world is about. Given a choice, people always do business with people they like and trust. If the urgent and trivial matters of the day are preventing the development of that very important part of your life, then how can the business grow? True recreation—doing the things you love to do—is needed to regenerate.

We're talking here not of the things you think you should do, only of the things you love to do. If walking is preferable to running, dancing better than swimming, listening to music at home more enjoyable than going out to a concert, then walk, dance and listen at home. Be good to yourself and you will feel your whole being regenerate.

In looking at the four listings of Stephen Covey's matrix, we can see how easily the activities of one, three and four prevent us from spending much time in two. But the fact is that spending a good part of our time in two is where the success of our business lies. Plan to be ruthless about your time; work towards your objectives and say firmly, "No, not now—but I can later", in a fair, effective and efficient way that suits your needs.

In support of your effective time management, whatever kind of business you're in, whatever the size of your company, good record keeping is important. You may not have the luxury of a full-time assistant, but you can be well organised all the same and have efficient methods for keeping track of essential information. The following suggestions might prove helpful:

Filing

If you deal with many different products, regions, departments or sales teams, it helps to colour-code your filing system. For example, each region would have a different colour file folder.

When you see, say, a yellow file folder in your "In" tray, you know at once that it concerns the northern region.

You will find files much more easily this way than by working through a stack of buff-coloured folders by reading their individual labels. Keep file labels the same colour as the folder, so you can go straight to the relevant folders when they are hanging together in the file cabinet.

Keep a few sheets of coloured paper in your personal organiser that correspond to the colours of your project files, so that you can write your notes on the appropriate paper and find them quickly in a meeting.

Business cards

Keep the business cards of clients and prospects even if you have entered the information elsewhere. At some future point, you may wish to refer to first-impression notes written on the back of the card. Also the style of the business card helps you get an idea of a company. Again you can use business cards to trace the progression of clients, based on the changes in their titles.

Date the card when the title changes, and you will have a paper trail. Keep the business cards of current clients or active prospects stapled onto the front or inside left of their file folders. If you deal with various people in the same organisation, staple all their cards there.

For those clients or prospective clients who do not yet have a file, cards can be kept in a binder containing plastic sheets with individual pockets for the cards. You can occasionally flip through your book to recall various people and perhaps produce new leads.

When a client or project is classified as "dead", remove the card from the active file folder and put it back into the general binder; you might want to refer to it again in the future. Never allow yourself to run out of your own business cards, and keep them clean and crisp in a leather case made for that purpose. These are available in stationery stores everywhere. No one likes to receive a creased or dog-eared business card, and a leather card case says a lot about you and your company.

Reading material

> *"An intellectual is a person whose mind watches itself."*
> Albert Camus (1913–1960)

If you're going to penetrate a business niche effectively by positioning yourself as the "expert company", you will want to stay on top of any and all information about your clients and their problems. Subscribe to all the magazines to which your clients subscribe.

Give a list of key words and topics to a junior staff person and assign that individual to the consistent task of clipping articles, highlighting them, colour-coding them to indicate in which category they should be filed and circulating them to the relevant staff.

This activity serves several purposes. First, it is a pipeline through which your staff can be kept fresh and vibrant, using the right jargon and conveying in every way to your clients that "we're the right company for you". Second, your assistant can separate the wheat from the chaff so that you won't be wasting valuable time reading articles from which there is nothing new to learn.

Third, culling through reading material helps that person learn, which in turn makes for a more valuable assistant. Finally, it is simpler to have a folder of relevant articles to take home with you at the end of the day or the week, rather than a heavy stack of magazines.

If magazine circulation within your company takes too long, consider subscribing to your own copy of really important publications. You lose your advantage if your information-gathering lags too far behind.

Make good organisational techniques work for you

> *"You know it is not a good wax museum when there are wicks coming out of people's heads."* Rick Reynolds

Reminder, Follow-up and To-Do Lists can save your business. List-making is an important component of staying sane. A computer software package that allows you or your assistant to keep a running list and to delete completed items is ideal.

If you don't have access to a computer, the following manual method might be a help: At the end of each day, prepare a To-Do list for the next day, highlighting the items that are a priority. At the end of the day, cross off the completed items and make up a new list for the next day.

To-Do lists can be kept in an organiser or a diary and the priorities should be clearly focused on achieving the objectives of your business and promotional plans. Everything else is probably just a distraction to those plans.

On Friday review the lists of that week to see what issues remain open. If you find that one issue keeps coming up on your list, decide whether it can be dropped altogether, or whether it must be dealt with now. If you have been procrastinating (and who doesn't?), make that item a priority for the next working day.

Names, addresses and other important information

Keep track of the names and addresses of (a) everybody you know or do business with, (b) people you hope to do business with and (c) potential contacts for the future. Make a note of each person's title. Remember to change the title when a promotion has taken place. Also note and keep the names and telephone numbers of people you contacted just once; even if they did not prove to be useful, they may well become so one day.

Note general and direct office numbers, fax numbers, e-mail and where appropriate, car phone numbers, beeper numbers, home and weekend house numbers, if these are offered.

Remember always that gatekeepers are important, helpful and

powerful. They like to be acknowledged as people, not just as objects on the other end of the telephone. Note a gatekeeper's name along with the name and other details of the client.

If you find that you remember the company's name more easily than the individual's name, file alphabetically by company name, and then by individual within the company. If you have met your client's spouse and children, make a note of their names in case you have occasion to meet or refer to them again.

With all this new-business activity, you may want a good software program to make life easier and more manageable. There are many packages available and you will want to determine the one that will best fit your needs. Talk to a number of people in similar businesses who use the same hardware as you do. Also visit the computer shows to discover the latest on the market.

Key points to remember

Manage your office work, staff and your time by focusing on your business plan objectives. Measure everything you do or are called upon to do by whether it contributes to the agreed goals or not.

How often have you heard major corporations blame their failure on the fact that they "took their eye off the ball for a minute"? Or they "got talked into it". Or "they felt that it would be a good deal because everyone else was going down that track". If your business plan and marketing plans are realistic, congruent, relevant and flexible, don't let anyone change your goals and pathways for any superficial unresearched reason.

> *"Destiny is not a matter of chance; it is a matter of choice. It is not a thing to be waited for; it is a thing to be achieved."* William Jennings Bryan

Step Eleven

Persistence pays

"I like life. It's something to do."	Ronnie Shakes

There is another very important step in this quest for winning new business, that of persistence. Almost anyone can put these steps into place, but not many people will keep on keeping on for days, weeks, months, years afterwards. Nothing replaces persistence. Persistence is what makes the other steps so powerful.

Perhaps it seems a formidable task to put our new-business system into place and it may be so at the beginning. However, the advantage of persistently pushing those barges down the canal is that you incorporate into your daily operations a system for bringing you continual new-business opportunities.

The expenditures for the process are the costs of your written materials, your telephone, and the time spent by your staff. The first mailing campaign may cost between three and five dollars per prospective client, depending on the size and quality of your initial mailing package.

The second and subsequent mailings can cost less or more, depending on your budget and your planned scale of inclusions. The commitment in time is a minimum of two years (in three-monthly cycles), a fairly standard time period given that the average closing-the-sale cycle is between fifteen and eighteen months.

In financial services, for instance, Shearson Lehman confirmed a statistic that I have also noted during my consulting years, that it takes around one hundred enquiries to convert five pieces of business over a period of about a year.

I found the same statistic true of executive recruiting in London. We had to visit one hundred companies before we found five really live possibilities, that is, companies that were unhappy enough with their current supplier to be prepared to move on. Even then, it took a year to eighteen months to get them settled into our organisation and get us up to handling them speedily and well. New business takes time.

Hotelier Willem Sprokkreeff was with the Hilton Group for many years and earned himself an awesome reputation for almost single-handedly dragging Australia's hospitality industry into quality performance.

After 35 years of total commitment to the Hilton Group, he retired and began consulting. At a recent meeting with him he said that he had found that it took two million dollars worth of promises to get two hundred thousand dollars worth of business. It ain't easy!

> *"It is courage the world needs, not infallibility ... courage is always the surest wisdom."* Sir Wilfred Grenfell

The sad thing is, so many salespeople think they are failures because they cannot close the sale instantly. About the only thing you can sell instantly is food and drink to a hungry and thirsty person at the only oasis in the desert! For the rest of us, it takes time, especially when the ticket item is high.

I have heard it estimated that replacing sales staff each year is a six billion dollar industry. Salespeople are hounded by management to close now, and because it does not happen that way, they become discouraged, and either resign or are sacked.

As Michael Hewitt-Gleeson points out, no-one can prove that there is any part of the human brain which can be manipulated into buying, even with a reward of $10,000, until such time as that human has established a real need to do so.

The mailing and phoning program for developing new business is a cost-effective, relationship-building marketing tool that lets you track the expenditures and the benefits on a month-by-month basis. It is a technique that can benefit almost any size or type of business or service company. You choose the clients you want in your business life and build trusting relationships, which lie at the heart of all business. The sale will follow.

Mailing and phoning around two hundred people over a

three-month (sixty working days) period means only a very few mailings and follow-up phone calls per day.

Never mail a huge amount all at once as you will get so far behind in trying to contact people for an appointment that you will be overwhelmed and stop trying. Instead, mail three or four each night and after an interval of about a week, phone those three or four people. If you don't reach them on the first try, try once more that day.

If you reach them, terrific! If you don't, send a note-card saying, "Sorry I missed you". Just keep moving. Do not get bogged down in worrying about the two hundred people as a whole. Simply see them as small lots of three or four mailings and a few phone calls per day.

Whether used together with other marketing strategies, or on its own, this program can be managed by an individual entrepreneur or by the secretary or assistant to the chief executive officer of a large company.

By making relationship-building with prospects a regular part of your business activities, not a once-a-year sales effort, you will always be in the middle of new-business building, whether times are good or bad. It is my belief that this is just the right solution for the present unpredictable climate.

> *"I like work; it fascinates me. I can sit and look at it for hours."* Jerome K. Jerome, 1859–1927

Key points to remember

Be persistent. Most people do not make even one business development phone call a day, regularly and relentlessly. They don't even work through sixty likely prospects over a three-month period.

It can be that easy: as low as one prospect a day will generate rewards. Three a day is fine, five a day is excellent, because multiplied by sixty working days in three months, you will have three hundred people you are phoning, sending cards and articles to, faxing, following up on.

When I contact my clients around the world and ask, "Of all the things we said and did together, what made the difference?"

without exception I get the reply, "Not feeling guilty for 91 days!"

Some days will be magic. Everything will flow, everything you touch will go well, life will be worth living after all. Then bang!—clients and customers complain, you have a fight with someone you love, your boss refuses your raise and your holiday leave . . .What happened? And what will you do?

One of two things. You can either react/resign/storm out and take it all personally or you can stand back and analyse, understand, shrug and move on. These people with whom you had trouble were probably under pressure.

When you know how they, and you, behave under pressure, you can understand the situation, handle it well and move on to other things. After all, it won't matter in a hundred years, you may murmur to yourself.

For an easier life all round, read the next step to understand how you can keep clients and prospects (and personal relationships) on more of an even keel.

Step Twelve

Keep your clients forever by understanding their personality styles

> *"People who think they know everything are very irritating to those of us who do."* Unknown

For me one of the most important aspects of success is understanding the different personalities. Why? Because I spent most of my life thinking that people were doing "it" to annoy me. Then I learned that people are different, that they do have their own reasons for their point of view and it is over to me to listen, to see their point of view and to accommodate their feelings and needs too.

The chart on the following page will help you determine how your personal style relates to the styles of your prospects, clients, friends, family and associates. Make a first pass at checking off the type you resemble the most. The people listed beside, over, or under your own square are the ones you are likely to handle best. The ones diagonally opposite are the ones with whom you are unlikely to get on in business.

Incidentally, people very often marry across the diagonals because they admire qualities in the other that they don't have themselves—though this may not be sufficient in the long term to hold the marriage together, judging by the divorce statistics.

Further on, there is a test on strengths and weaknesses, which will help you make a definite decision as to your personality profile and that of clients and prospects. You may be interested in using the test with family and friends, too, so as to understand them better.

Four Main Profiles

Enquirers

(Chief accountant types) Need lots of detail; like to have everything on file. Until they trust you, they award projects only; then they award the entire job.

Workspace is activity-oriented. Walls may be decorated with diplomas and other marks of achievement. Office is organised and work-oriented. Contact between people is businesslike.

Aspirers

(Entrepreneurial types) Brisk, to the point, want the whole picture now. They admire efficiency, speed; make decisions rapidly, without proper research.

Efficiency is the theme. Walls may have an appropriate picture or achievement award but no posters or slogans. Office is activity-oriented with a lot of work materials. Desk may be in a dominant position.

Admirers

(Human resources types) Warm, friendly, chatty, need to talk for at least 20 minutes before getting down to business.

You will get their business if you are "one of them", and your service benefits the people of their organisation.

Overall atmosphere is friendly and open. Look for posters and personal items on walls and desks. Office is neat and functional. Contact between people is open. Family photos may abound.

Inspirers

(Visionaries, heads of big companies) Have big ideas, need lots of variety, are easily bored, don't like to be bothered with detail.

You will get their business if you delight them with your humour, brilliance, good sense of fun.

General theme is about motivation. Walls may be covered with posters and slogans. Atmosphere is friendly and open. Desk may look cluttered and disorganised. Contact between people is open.

Your personality profile—strengths

Please mark off one word on each line **across** that you feel most aptly describes you at work. Don't think too long, just do it as quickly and as honestly as you can.

1.	Animated	Persuasive	Planner	Adaptable
2.	Refreshing	Sure	Orderly	Peaceful
3.	Cheerful	Daring	Idealistic	Submissive
4.	Demonstrative	Adventurous	Perfectionist	Considerate
5.	Bouncy	Independent	Self-sacrificing	Respectful
6.	Playful	Decisive	Controlled	Satisfied
7.	Spontaneous	Tenacious	Sensitive	Patient
8.	Delightful	Chieftain	Faithful	Shy
9.	Sociable	Bold	Musical	Obliging
10.	Outspoken	Competitive	Loyal	Friendly
11.	Funny	Self-reliant	Analytical	Diplomatic
12.	Talkative	Positive	Persistent	Consistent
13.	Convincing	Mover	Reserved	Inoffensive
14.	Spirited	Leader	Scheduled	Dry humour
15.	Promoter	Productive	Cultured	Mediator
16.	Inspiring	Strong-willed	Mapmaker	Tolerant
17.	Mixes easily	Resourceful	Balanced	Listener
18.	Cute	Optimistic	Detailed	Contented
19.	Popular	Forceful	Thoughtful	Permissive
20.	Lively	Confident	Deep	Well-behaved
*	....	....	....	....
	Inspirer (Visionary type, corporate head)	Aspirer (Entrepreneur type)	Enquirer (Accountant type)	Admirer (Human resources type)

Add up the number of **words** you have ticked in each column and write the final count in the space above*

Your personality profile—weaknesses

Answer on the basis of how you behave at work.

Move as quickly and as honestly as you can through the possibilities listed. Tick one only in each line across.

1.	Brassy	Impatient	Reluctant	Fussy
2.	Undisciplined	Unpopular	Plain ordinary	Too sensitive
3.	Naive	Headstrong	Worrier	Doubtful
4.	Inconsistent	Angers easily	Low energies	Loner
5.	Messy	Bossy	Sluggish	Insecure
6.	Haphazard	Unsympathetic	Revengeful	Pessimistic
7.	Disorganised	Resentful	Compromising	Negative
8.	Forgetful	Tactless	Fearful	Withdrawn
9.	Unpredictable	Stubborn	Uninvolved	Moody
10.	Argumentative	Lordly	Suspicious	Selfish

11. Show-off	Restless	Introvert	Critical
12. Interruptive	Proud	Indecisive	Hard to please
13. Permissive	Edgy/nervy	Timid	Slow to respond
14. Wants credit	Workaholic	Mumbles	Unaffectionate
15. Talkative	Domineering	Lazy	Alienated
16. Loud	Intolerant	Blank	Indifferent
17. Scatterbrain	Short-tempered	Unforgiving	Sceptical
18. Rash	Crafty	Hesitant	Bashful
19. Changeable	Manipulative	Nonchalant	Unenthusiastic
20. Resistant	Frank	Depressed	Repetitious
*	....	....	....
Inspirer Visionary	Aspirer Entrepreneur	Enquirer Accountant	Admirer Human Resources

Add up the number of words you have ticked in each column and write the final count in the space above*

Your combined strengths and weaknesses scores

....	....	....	....
Inspirer Visionary	Aspirer Entrepreneur	Enquirer Accountant	Admirer Human Resources

Now that you have combined the scores for the strengths and weaknesses of each personality style, you will see that your most dominant style is the column with the top mark. Your backup style is your next highest score.

Although a person may be fairly evenly spread among three, or even all four styles, the usual result is to be very strongly one or two.

Your second highest score, your backup style, tends to be the one you revert to in your spare time when the serious work of the week is over.

You can use the same analysis to define your clients, customers and prospects, but you may find it easier to begin with people you know well: friends, lovers, spouse, children, workmates.

See if this profile analysis helps you to understand why your differing strengths attract them and your weaknesses annoy them.

Here is the same chart again for you to make as many copies as you need. The more you practise, the more you will understand and adapt.

Personality profile—strengths

Person's name ....

Mark off one word on each line across that you feel most aptly describes this person.

1.	Animated	Persuasive	Planner	Adaptable
2.	Refreshing	Sure	Orderly	Peaceful
3.	Cheerful	Daring	Idealistic	Submissive
4.	Demonstrative	Adventurous	Perfectionist	Considerate
5.	Bouncy	Independent	Self-sacrificing	Respectful
6.	Playful	Decisive	Controlled	Satisfied
7.	Spontaneous	Tenacious	Sensitive	Patient
8.	Delightful	Chieftain	Faithful	Shy
9.	Sociable	Bold	Musical	Obliging
10.	Outspoken	Competitive	Loyal	Friendly
11.	Funny	Self-reliant	Analytical	Diplomatic
12.	Talkative	Positive	Persistent	Consistent
13.	Convincing	Mover	Reserved	Inoffensive
14.	Spirited	Leader	Scheduled	Dry humour
15.	Promoter	Productive	Cultured	Mediator
16.	Inspiring	Strong-willed	Mapmaker	Tolerant
17.	Mixes easily	Resourceful	Balanced	Listener
18.	Cute	Optimistic	Detailed	Contented
19.	Popular	Forceful	Thoughtful	Permissive
20.	Lively	Confident	Deep	Well-behaved
*	....	....	....	....
	Inspirer	Aspirer	Enquirer	Admirer
	Visionary	Entrepreneur	Accountant	Human Resources

Add up the number of words you have ticked in each column and write the final count in the space above*

Now on to weaknesses:

Personality profile—weaknesses

Person's name ....

Mark off one word on each line across that you feel most aptly describes this person.

1.	Brassy	Impatient	Reluctant	Fussy
2.	Undisciplined	Unpopular	Plain ordinary	Too sensitive
3.	Naive	Headstrong	Worrier	Doubtful
4.	Inconsistent	Angers easily	Low energies	Loner
5.	Messy	Bossy	Sluggish	Insecure
6.	Haphazard	Unsympathetic	Revengeful	Pessimistic
7.	Disorganised	Resentful	Compromising	Negative
8.	Forgetful	Tactless	Fearful	Withdrawn
9.	Unpredictable	Stubborn	Uninvolved	Moody
10.	Argumentative	Lordly	Suspicious	Selfish
11.	Show-off	Restless	Introvert	Critical
12.	Interruptive	Proud	Indecisive	Hard to please
13.	Permissive	Edgy/nervy	Timid	Slow to respond
14.	Wants credit	Workaholic	Mumbles	Unaffectionate
15.	Talkative	Domineering	Lazy	Alienated
16.	Loud	Intolerant	Blank	Indifferent
17.	Scatterbrain	Short-tempered	Unforgiving	Sceptical
18.	Rash	Crafty	Hesitant	Bashful
19.	Changeable	Manipulative	Nonchalant	Unenthusiastic
20.	Resistant	Frank	Depressed	Repetitious
*	....	....	....	....
	Inspirer Visionary	Aspirer Entrepreneur	Enquirer Accountant	Admirer Human Resources

Add up the number of words you have ticked in each column and write the final count in the space above*

Combine strengths and weaknesses scores below.

....

Inspirer	Aspirer	Enquirer	Admirer
Visionary	Entrepreneur	Accountant	Human Resources

Remember that people can behave differently at work and at home. We all have a backup style which comes into play as we leave the office.

And now for more information on these various personality styles and how they behave as client, customer or prospect.

Aspirers (entrepreneurs) as clients

> *"A team effort is a lot of people doing what I say."*
> Michael Winner, British film director

Codenames: **The extrovert, the talker, the optimist.**

They want the whole picture now, together with organisation, practical solutions and quick action.

They delegate readily when others have proved absolutely trustworthy, but insist on goal and time setting. They thrive on opposition, have little need for friends, are usually right (!) and excel in emergencies.

Strengths: Dynamic, active, good at correcting wrongs, not easily discouraged, exude confidence, can run anything, have a strong need for change, born to lead.

Weaknesses: Not very tolerant of mistakes/fools, do not analyse detail, make rash decisions, are bored by trivia, may be rude and tactless, are demanding, believe the end justifies the means.

Enquirers (accountants) as clients

> *"The volume of paper expands to fill the available briefcases."*
> Jerry Brown

Codenames: **The introvert, the pessimist, the thinker**.

They are schedule-oriented, perfectionists and detail-conscious. Orderly and organised, they hunt for economical solutions and they like graphs, charts, figures and lists.

Strengths: Deep, thoughtful, analytical, serious, purposeful, talented, creative, beauty-loving, self-sacrificing, idealistic, sensitive.

Weaknesses: Prone to choose difficult work, not people-oriented, hesitant about starting projects, hard to please with standards that are often too high, critical of others, need approval badly, hold back affection, dislike opposition, suspicious and unforgiving, martyr-prone, tend to hypochondria.

Admirers (human resources types) as clients

> *"Agree, for the law is costly."*
> William Camden, 1551–1623

Codenames: **The introvert, the watcher, the pessimist.**

They are competent and steady, peaceful and agreeable, with good administrative abilities. They avoid conflict, solve problems and come into their own under pressure. They are good listeners, have many friends and contacts, are compassionate and concerned, quick to look for the easiest way.

Strengths: Low-key in personality, easygoing, relaxed, cool, calm and collected, persistent, well-balanced, patient, quiet, witty, able to hide emotions. An all-purpose type, they make good clients because they can take the good with the bad and do not get upset easily. Since they are not in too much of a hurry, you have time to do a good job for them.

Weaknesses: Unenthusiastic, indecisive, tend to avoid responsibility, selfish, self-righteous, too compromising yet resentful about being pushed, sometimes lazy, prefer to watch rather than participate, tend to dampen enthusiasm, lack discipline, can be sarcastic and teasing.

Inspirers (visionaries, heads of large organisations) as clients

> *"The scientific theory I like best is that the rings of Saturn are composed entirely of lost airline baggage."*
> Mark Russell

Codenames: **The extrovert, the talker, the optimist.**

They apologise readily, do not hold a grudge, thrive on compliments. They love spontaneous activities and lots of people, are open to big ideas, anxious to make you feel at home, quick to think up new activities and projects, creative and colourful, bursting with energy and enthusiasm.

Strengths: They have an excellent sense of humour, are the life of the party, emotional, enthusiastic, expressive, curious, now-centred but quick to change disposition, always a child, always good at heart.

Weaknesses: Forgetful of names and obligations, undisciplined, off-putting by reason of their huge energy and enthusiasm; tend not to follow through, talk and laugh loudly, are easily distracted, quick to interrupt, wasteful of time, apt to confuse priorities, then lose confidence easily, are naive, keep the office in a frenzy.

Ways we can modify our own behaviour

> *"When down in the mouth, remember Jonah. He came out alright."* Thomas Edison, 1847–1931

Now that we know our strengths and weaknesses, what do we do to make our dealings with other people more effective?

Aspirers (entrepreneurs) maintain a high-assertive, low-responsive behaviour, want to stick to their business and work independently.

They tend to be blunt, overbearing, competitive and impatient, wanting to control situations and people. If you are an Aspirer, appropriate behaviour modifications would be to:
—develop empathy;
—learn to relax and pace yourself;
—be willing to listen and understand the feelings of others.
—develop patience.

Enquirers (accountants) maintain a low-assertive, low-responsive behaviour, want to stick to the facts and get down to business without any chitchat. They follow procedures to the letter, are very conservative and analytical, resistant to change. If you are an Enquirer, appropriate behaviour modifications would be to:
—develop an understanding of the importance of feelings;
—learn to make decisions based on intuition and facts;

—be willing to bend the rules to accommodate others;
—take the initiative.

Admirers (human resources) maintain low-assertive, low-responsive behaviour. They beat around the bush in an effort to be kind and tolerant of others and take deliberate actions based on feelings and relationships. They can be lazy, sarcastic and teasing. If you are an Admirer, appropriate behaviour modifications would be to:
—develop a sense of urgency;
—learn self-assertion and strength of convictions;
—be willing to take the initiative;
—think before letting fly with sarcasm.

Inspirers (visionaries, heads of large organisations) maintain a high-assertive, high-responsive behaviour. They can be over-enthusiastic, over-optimistic and too hyped up. Their quick action is generally based on feelings and relationships. If you are an Inspirer, appropriate behaviour modifications would be to:
—develop emotional control;
—learn to use work time more wisely;
—be willing to analyse data and pay attention to facts;
—be objective.

Strategies for dealing with the four main personality styles

> *"Happiness is good health and a bad memory."*
> Ingrid Bergman (1917–1982)

Aspirers (entrepreneurs)

1. **Initiating contact with Aspirers:** Aspirers seldom read introductory letters. Make your initial contact by phone. Your call should be businesslike and to the point. Introduce yourself, explain why you are calling and ask for an appointment. Confirm the meeting by letter and enclose any pre-meeting information the Aspirers request.

2. **Relating to Aspirers:** Aspirers value punctuality and efficient use of time. Be on time. Use factual evidence to establish your company's competence, get down to business in a formal manner. When Aspirers speak, focus your attention on their ideas and goals. Listen carefully and use facts only when answering any questions. Do not waste time, leave immediately business is done.
3. **Asking questions to discover Aspirers' needs:** Ask questions that are fact/results-oriented. Keep your questions open-ended and listen to the response; you won't be told twice. Support their conclusions and confirm their needs by feeding back your understanding—factually and clearly. Don't mumble, stutter, and "hope for the best"!
4. **Showing why Aspirers should use your company:** Be specific, but don't overwhelm them with details. Offer alternative solutions and let Aspirers make their own decision from the options. One solution is not enough, they need an either/or situation.

   But don't do as I did once: I took in eight possible solutions to a woman whom I now know to be an Aspirer. She was really quite angry to have to waste her time working through so many choices. No more than three, ever, was her cry! (An Inspirer, however, might have liked the fun of debating all eight alternatives!)
5. **Supporting Aspirers' use of your company:** Let Aspirers make their decision by asking directly for their business. Be prepared to reply with facts to any concerns they have and to be clear about alternative ways of meeting their company's needs. Be willing to negotiate regarding their ideas and objectives.

Enquirers (accountants)

1. **Initiating contact with Enquirers:** Start with a personal letter which gives specific information about your company. Be sure to include information about your company's background and expertise, stability and cost-effectiveness. Follow the letter with a phone call requesting a meeting. A businesslike manner, stating how much time you will need and what you will bring with you, works well with these people.
2. **Relating to Enquirers:** Be on time. State your purpose for the visit and stick to your agenda. Enquirers will want evidence of your company's problem-solving abilities. Present your evidence in a careful and deliberate manner.

3. **Asking questions to discover Enquirers' needs:** Ask specific "how" and "what" questions and make copious notes on the answers. Take an unhurried approach. Encourage them to relate their feelings as to "what" it is they are trying to achieve and "how" it is important to the company. Summarise those factors indicated as important and be prepared for additional discussions on these matters.
4. **Showing why Enquirers should use your company:** Prepare a well-organised, detailed, written plan which offers logical, systematic approaches. Emotional appeals will not work with Enquirers. Use examples to show how your proposal will solve their particular problems. If they ask a question you cannot answer, offer to find out and get back to them. Do not pretend to know, they will sense it immediately.
5. **Supporting Enquirers' use of your company:** Use a low-key approach to ask for the order. Concerns should be addressed by appealing to their sense of value-for-money and objectivity. Be prepared to negotiate details and probably price. If you cannot yield on price now, offer a value-added deal such as a discount on payment within five working days, or volume discount after so many "done deals".

Admirers (human resources)

1. **Initiating contact with Admirers:** Initial contact should be made through a letter of introduction stating who you are and why you are writing. Be sure to include information about your reputation, reliability and experience as well as the quality of your company's service. Follow the letter with a phone call. Take time to be friendly and establish a trusting relationship before asking for a meeting.
2. **Relating to Admirers:** Start the meeting on time with friendly chitchat intended to establish your relationship. Admirers will be most interested in information about you and want you to be genuinely interested in information about them. Initiate the business discussion by describing how you will work to solve their problems.
3. **Asking questions to discover Admirers' needs:** Ask open-ended questions which will draw out their personal goals and needs. Clarify their feelings in your own mind by asking "what" and "when" questions. Admirers will expect you to listen actively by giving plenty of verbal and non-verbal feedback. When summarising, reflect your understanding of their concerns and feelings.

4. **Showing why Admirers should use your company:** Provide a clear, written solution to their needs, indicating how you will work together. They must be assured that your solution will work, now and in the future. Personally guarantee your proposal. Admirers will also want to know what other people think of your work, so give them the names of people they can contact, together with phone numbers, titles, company names.
5. **Supporting Admirers' use of your company:** Don't back Admirers into a corner or try to force them to make a decision. Ask for the business in an indirect manner. Listen to their concerns in a patient, peaceful way and give calm, thorough answers. The Admirer will try to avoid making a commitment, so be sure to stress your personal involvement in follow-up activities.

Inspirers (visionaries)

1. **Initiating contact with Inspirers:** Start with a phone call. To Inspirers, letters are impersonal and usually go unread. The tone of your phone call should be open and friendly. Stress your experience, personal service and (quickly) the benefits of using your company.
2. **Relating to Inspirers:** Be on time yourself but be prepared to wait for the Inspirer—they have no use for clockwatchers. They have plenty of time for small talk and will want to build a personal relationship by swapping stories about mutual acquaintances. Get them to talk about their personal interests (an easy task) and relate your own feelings.
3. **Asking questions to discover Inspirers' needs:** Questions to Inspirers should be direct and probing, using "who", "what", "how". Show an active interest in their responses by providing a lot of verbal and non-verbal feedback. Your questions should help you gain specific information about their goals. As you summarise, relate your own feelings while bringing goals and needs into sharp focus.
4. **Showing why Inspirers should use your company**: Be specific and factual but do not overwhelm them with a lot of detail. Try to keep the discussion on track without pushing too hard. Work closely to develop ideas and strategies. Inspirers are easily bored so do not stay on one subject too long. They have no problem with accommodating five or ten ideas at one time and are wonderful candidates for an exciting and vibrant meeting.

5. **Supporting Inspirers' use of your company:** Always assume that you have the contract. Concerns should be dealt with by sharing stories of other people's successes through using your company. Give exciting, alive case studies, quick and to the point. Make the incentive you offer a bright, new way of looking at old, dull and boring contracts. For instance, when they reach a certain level of dollars spent with your company, you offer extra product free, as opposed to, say, a volume discount.

   Or give a volume discount based on an estimate of a year's buying needs. If they reach that volume, fine; if not, they owe you. However, if they go beyond that volume you owe them money.

   I have used this technique very successfully in the hotel industry. It worked so well with a good-sized supplier of room nights to the Inter-Continental Hotel where I was sales manager, that we owed them enough money to guarantee that their volume per night room rate stayed the same for the whole of the following year. They preferred this type of refund to actual cash in hand. It turned a very average relationship into a very successful one for both parties.

> *"Even if you're on the right track, you'll get run over if you just sit there."* Will Rogers (1879–1935)

How the four types behave under stress

> *"It is easier to get forgiveness than permission."*
> Murphy's Law, Book 2 (P.S. O'Halloran's Law says Murphy's Laws are optimistic)

Be aware that each of us, in addition to our dominant personality style, has a hidden profile which shows itself under great stress or tension. Back-up profiles are characterised by immature reactions and behaviour.

When they are in evidence, all you can do is focus on leading that angry, upset client, prospect, friend or family member through the tension and back into the dominant personality style you are used to. **Do not take it personally. You are sorry that it happened, but it is not your fault.**

Aspirers (entrepreneurs) will behave like "Der Fuhrer". Aspirers like to be in control, but never more so than when stressed out. They will coldly snap out orders and decisions with no room for discussion. Facts and logic will support their rage. The best way to deal with Der Fuhrer is to listen to the complaints with empathy and intelligent responses. Once they see that their feelings carry weight with you, you will be able to get them back to their normal Aspirer behaviour. You have shown them that they are in charge and that their decisions and feelings are important.

Enquirers (accountants) will become a sullen act. Their basic tendency to avoid making decisions now spreads over into all areas: they just won't deal with anything. They become curt and surly, refusing to answer questions and cutting short your responses. Give them permission to speak out and say what is wrong. Simply listen. Allow them an opportunity to let off steam—and be prepared for a torrent! Agree with their feelings and offer alternatives based on some new information.

Admirers (human resources) become doormats. They deal with conflict by lying down. They will sign anything, do anything if you will just go away and leave them alone. You can expect a call later, however, cancelling the contract. When the Admirer stops discussing things with you and says, "Fine, do it any way you want", take time out to find out what is wrong. Suggest they dump on you and be prepared for a blazing personal attack. Anything and everything is open to attack.

Inspirers (visionaries) become spoilt brats who are displeased with everything and anything around them. They can be rude, uncooperative, blunt and angry with you, your work, your tie or dress even. Let them wear themselves out, and show that you relate to their feelings. Nod empathetically. When the storm is over, get on with working together in a way that meets their needs. They will forgive you over a great lunch and your note of apology goes a long way.

Make the four main personality profiles work for you

Underneath the headings of the four personality styles, list as many of your clients and prospects as you can fit in. Remind yourself that these are the people you deal with on a daily basis.

Aspirers (entrepreneurs) ....

....

....

....

Enquirers (accountants) ....

....

....

....

Admirers (human resources) ....

....

....

....

Inspirers (visionaries, heads of large organisations) ....

....

....

....

NLP—Neurolinguistic programming—the three languages of seeing, hearing and feeling

> *"We must believe in luck, for how else can we explain the success of those we don't like?"* Jean Cocteau (1889–1963)

The number-one secret weapon for transferring information effectively is to adapt your personal communications style to that of your audience.

Neurolinguistic programming (NLP) was discovered by the famed psychoanalyst Carl Jung. He found, through listening to his patients tell their life stories, that we humans have three different styles of communicating, each with its own matching spoken and written language.

These styles are **visual** where we express ourselves largely in pictures, **auditory** where we use hard-nosed facts, and **feelings** where we speak of how we felt.

These styles enable us to communicate easily with those like us and can hinder us from communicating well with others who are not like us. As a result you may have said, felt and heard these comments often, where your personal communications style has not matched those of the recipients:

- "He just doesn't speak our language."
- "No matter how often I tell them, they just don't listen."
- "It's like talking to a blank wall."
- "They just don't get it."
- "None so blind as those who will not see."
- "It seems as though they are totally deaf."
- "There's nothing except blank indifference."
- "They're just not in touch with the issues."

These personal styles operate on a 40/20/40 rule of thumb:

- Forty per cent of people see pictures as you talk to them, and use highly visual language when speaking and writing, such as:
  "I can see the whole picture now."
  "I saw Jim last week."
  "See you soon."
  "I want to show you this . . ."
  "Look here."
  "See what I mean?"
- Twenty per cent of people respond best to auditory words and use sound-oriented words in their speech and when they write, such as:
  "I hear you loud and clear."
  "I spoke with Jim last week."
  "Talk to you soon."
  "Come and talk to me."
  "That rings a bell."
  "Let's talk this through."

- Forty per cent of people respond to feeling words, and use sensitive words in their speaking and writing, such as:
  "I feel very deeply on this issue."
  "I touched base with Jim last week."
  "Let's get together soon."
  "This is a sensitive issue."
  "How do you feel about this?"
  "Stay in touch, if it's not too much trouble."

A real-life example: friend Jo had written a letter of complaint to a department store and received a quick phone response. The company representative said, "I can feel your anger". Jo was deeply insulted—she is among that twenty per cent that responds to auditory language, not that forty per cent that responds through their feelings.

I asked Jo how she would have felt if the caller had said, "I hear your anger", and Jo agreed that would be fine. How about, "I can see that you are angry"? I asked. That would have been okay as well. Most people have a backup language and Jo's primary style is auditory with a backup style of visual. Yet, even understanding what was going on, Jo swore she would never shop at that store again.

Yes, it can be that easy to lose a sale or further upset a customer or client.

It's also a good idea to use neutral language when seeking an appointment. Ask only if you can meet, not "have an appointment to see . . ."; not "I have a feeling we should get together"; not "I think we should talk". Use language that does not trigger negative responses and your ratio of appointments to phone calls could well improve. Or you could use all three languages when asking for an appointment by saying, "How do you feel about my coming to see you and talking through your needs?"

Another example: imagine for a moment that three people go to visit Janet, their office manager, who has broken her leg skiing. A visual person would report back that they had great fun drawing graffiti on her cast. A hearing person, that they knocked on the cast and it sounded hollow—Janet is disappearing inside. A feeling person, that Janet is going nuts with the itchy bits inside. Same person, same cast, three different opinions, behaviours and reactions.

The second clue to the communications style of people with whom you're speaking is in their eye movement. People who are asked to remember a past occasion look up towards their eyebrows if they hear by seeing, as if seeing the picture of the previous event in their mind's eye. If they respond by hearing, they look sideways toward their ears to hear the words of that time. If they hear by feeling, they look down toward their hearts to recapture the emotions of that time.

For instance Bob Hawke was thought to be shifty because his eyes went sideways to his ears when he was recalling what was said or done in the past. He was simply looking for the sound, not avoiding or lying about the issue.

Several people involved in executive recruitment remarked to me recently that they had always judged applicants to be shifty when they looked sideways before answering interview questions. Now they realise it is a recall mode. Eyes moving up into the eyebrows or down into the heart for visual and feeling recall do not create the same shifty impression; if noticed at all, they are simply seen as normal eye movements.

Of course, if you are making a presentation to a room full of people, you can't watch them all for these clues and still remember what you're trying to say. Therefore, make sure your presentation addresses each communication style. Add more descriptive words and sounds into your verbal presentations, include relevant background music and sounds; try to capture the eyes, ears, hearts (and minds) of one hundred per cent of your listeners.

Otherwise you can lose between sixty and eighty per cent of your listeners by using your own preferred speaking style. Adjust to your audience as you would try to do in a foreign country. If you want to eat, sleep, fill up the car, buy medical supplies or ask directions, it really helps if you know the words in their language. Suddenly it is so easy.

In the same way our presentations come alive for all those people sitting there, judging our best work. By using all of the three languages of your audience, you enrol the whole room rather than a small part. It has been said that usually about twenty-five per cent of the room are listening, the other seventy-five per cent are somewhere between apathy and deep dislike. No longer—now you can have one hundred per cent of people listening, empathising and buying into your presentations.

For example, you are presenting an advertising campaign for "Janna's" new range of leisure wear linked to an outdoor lifestyle. Perhaps you will be showing boards with pictures on them, to represent your TV campaign. Your storyboards would show people wearing Janna's leisure clothes against the backdrop of Sydney's Harbour Bridge, Opera House and waterways, enhanced by trains, ships, small craft and racing yachts. Or you could use an anamatic, being lively drawings on video. Either way, a voice tells the story. And of course the clothes are on show—it is very visual at this stage.

If you were a person with a visual communication style you would probably automatically use this kind of visual language to describe the TV commercial:

"The glitter of the speeding trains on the bridge, the cool whiteness of the Opera House under the bright sun, the colourful yachts under full spinnaker and the waves foaming around the bow . . . Janna's leisure wear is seen to its best advantage."

If hearing language came naturally to you, you would perhaps talk of "the clickety-clack of the trains, the sound of the music in the Opera House, the hiss of the waves as the yachts cut through the water, racing to the starting line, and the crack and slap of the sails as they change direction . . . Janna's leisure wear captures the applause of the weekend set."

And if you were someone who naturally used feeling language, you might talk about "being on the most beautiful harbour in the world, close to the great performers at the Opera House; the delight of the wind in our hair and the sun on our faces as we hold the tiller, fighting for the starting position . . . Janna's leisure wear has that certain feeling."

Now here is an example of how you can use all three languages at once to enrol the whole audience in your pitch:

"As the silver train clatters across the bridge, a vista unfolds. The Opera House gleams white in the bright Sydney sun, the famous voices within echoing in our minds. Yachts under brightly coloured spinnakers speed to the line. The boom of the starting gun tells us the race is on. We can taste the salt on our lips, feel the wind in our hair, the sun on our faces. A great lifestyle invites us in as we see, hear and feel the pleasure of Janna's new collection."

Backed by the right music, interspersed with the clickety-clack of trains, the voices of famous opera singers, the hiss of the waves, the starting-gun shot, your presentation will now involve everyone in the room, and particularly those who respond with their ears.

These people are the most difficult of all to sway, these twenty per cent! They truly have to hear it to believe it. Then of course the others have to see it to believe and have to feel that the campaign is right for the product.

> *"Some things have to be believed to be seen."*
> Ralph Hodgson on ESP

What makes a golden oldie?

Why do some songs go on and on and others die before they fly? Can it be something to do with the three languages with which they communicate? Is it that there is something in the song for all of us? For an example of a true golden oldie, let's look at a song from *My Fair Lady*.

"I have often **walked** down this street before
But the pavement always stayed beneath my feet before
All at once am I **several storeys high**
Knowing I'm on the street where you live.
Are there lilac trees in the heart of town
Can you **hear a lark** in any other part of town
Does enchantment pour out of every door
No, it's just on the street where you live
An **overpowering feeling**
Just to know somehow that you are near
The **overpowering feeling**
That any second you may suddenly **appear**
People stop and **stare**
They don't **bother** me
For there is nowhere else I would rather be
Let the time go by
I won't care if I can be
On the street where you live. "

I have marked in bold the three languages of this song, with "walked", and "hear a lark", being auditory language. Visual language shows in, "several storeys high", "enchantment pour out of every door", and "stare". Feeling language is throughout the song, particularly in, "Overpowering feeling" (repeated), "bother", and "won't care".

Now you can have fun predicting how long new songs will remain at the top of the charts. Analyse them for the weighting of the three languages and see if the songs richer in all three last longer.

Neurolinguistics and new business

During a recent pitch, I knew that two out of the three people in the room were entirely with me. The third was sitting back in his chair, arms folded, frowning in disbelief. I had been talking about the importance of NLP in helping to win new business, but John was not convinced.

"What is my style?" he asked. Because it was a small group, I had managed to pick up his eye movements, so I replied that he was possibly auditory.

"How will you convince me?" he demanded. I replied, "By giving you the names and numbers of people that you can phone, so that you can hear through your ears that this technique is successful."

A moment of silence, then he laughed, and I now had three people in the room who were in agreement with me.

It's not so difficult to use all three language styles at once if you are already a good communicator.

Neurolinguistics and your personal life

Let's consider "Love Strategies" for analysing what makes you and others feel truly loved.

The study of neurolinguistics shows us that when we fall in love we use all three languages at the same time. We see love in our beloved's eye, and they in ours, we bring gifts, we whisper sweet nothings and oh, the towering feeling of the hugs, the love-making, the nibbling and stroking.

Then time goes by and it's no longer the same; it seems that love has died. Why? Because after the first flush of excitement, each of us reverts to our preferred and backup styles. If our partner has the same styles, all is well because we settle well into friendship and mutual respect. Otherwise we break up, move on, looking again for that special person who will understand us, make us feel loved again. Or else we stay, wishing things were different but without the skills to know what the problem is.

For instance a highly feeling man will long for hugs, for touch; his highly visual partner will long for flowers, for little gifts. An auditory woman will say, "He no longer loves me"—the proof being that he doesn't tell her so any more.

Recently I spoke to a young woman, now divorced. I asked her what went wrong. She explained that as her husband came home from work, he made a beeline for her. She, with three children underfoot wanting their dinner, dreaded his arrival.

Her comment was, "He couldn't even **see** that I was trying to get dinner and do you know, he never even **brought me a flower from my own garden**". A highly feeling man with a highly visual woman—and had either of them known what was going on, they might have compromised. He with a flower before dinner, she with affection after dinner.

Here we have a couple of lost people wondering why it wasn't working after being so in love only a few years ago. I asked her husband what went wrong and he said, **"She never said please, she just told me to do things"**. It hurt his feelings to be "told"—and since he didn't bring her flowers, they got divorced.

Let me tell you about the love strategy of a young woman volunteer at a seminar in Sydney. Up on the stage in front of 1200 people, Tony Robbins asked her what had to happen for her to feel absolutely loved. Did she have to see it in the eyes of her beloved, in the gifts that he brought. No. Did she have to hear it in the words that he said. No. Did she have to feel it in a certain way. YES!

What was that certain way? She explained that "he" would have to come to her, place his fingertips over her cupped, upward-facing fingers, then oh! so gently put his arms around her and hold her to him. Then she would feel absolutely loved.

Assuming that she was no longer with that man who made her feel so loved, how much chance would she have of ever feeling loved by another man—unless that man happened to be in the audience that night!

So what is your love strategy? Think back to a time when you felt absolutely loved or loving. Did you have to see it, to hear it, or to feel it? Many of us would say all three, yet there is usually one that you could not bear to be without.

Would you give up the shining, loving look in their eyes for words and a hug? Perhaps, perhaps not.

Would you give up the words, "I love you", for the gifts, the shining eyes, the hugs? Perhaps, perhaps not.

Would you give up the hugs for words, for gifts, for loving eyes? Perhaps, perhaps not.

When you have identified your preferred way of being loved, ask yourself if you know your partner's—and if not, what would change if you did. I know a woman whose husband brings her flowers every Friday night, and every Friday night there is a special dinner cooked, just for the two of them.

And remember too that every person you meet in business or in friendship has a preferred way of feeling loved. They too have the emotional needs that you and I have. They may like little gifts, or they may feel "bought".

They may like to hear words of admiration or they may feel manipulated.

They may like a warm touch, or they may feel affronted. It may sound like a minefield, but people send out signals all the time. Now that you are receptive to these signals the answers will come through loud and clear; you will see and feel what is going on. Remember when we were children and we sniffed the breeze on arriving home. We knew instantly what mood the adults were in, how we should adapt in order to survive! You can do it now that you are an adult—the skills are still there, just waiting to be used again.

Testing yourself for your preferred neurolinguistic style

> *"Tradition is what you resort to when you don't have the time or the money to do it right."*
>
> Kurt Herbert Adler, 1905–1988

The following phrases are commonly used in speaking and writing, depending on whether a person takes in information by seeing in pictures, by hearing the words or by feeling the meaning of what is being said. In each of the three columns, mark off the phrases you most commonly use. Your natural style is the column with the greatest number marked off.

Most people have a secondary style and some use all three. If you range across all three almost equally, congratulations!—you are a natural-born communicator. The rest of us need to practise using more of the words we are short on, in order to enrol the rest of the world when we speak.

There is a fourth style called "gustatory", which slips into the languages of the other three now and then.

The NLP language of seeing

Get an eyeful of this
It **appears** to me
I turn a **blind eye**
I got a **bird's-eye view**
Catch a **glimpse** of this
It's **crystal** clear
I take a **dim view** of that
See you soon
I **see** what you mean
When did I last **see** you?
In **light** of the new information
In my mind's **eye**
Paint me a **picture**
Show me what you mean
Let me **see** the facts
It is a **far-sighted** approach
He has tunnel **vision**

The NLP language of hearing

Tell me what you think
Do I **hear** you saying
I **hear** you loud and clear
I **bent** his ear
That **rings a bell**
To **tell** the truth
He was quite **deaf** to my **commands**
I totally **switched off**
We repeated it **word for word**
They were well **informed**
There was a hidden **message**
You are not **listening** to me
When did I last **hear** from you?
I turned a **deaf ear**
Speak to me
Call me in the morning
Come and **talk** to me

How many did you mark off?

A client recently quoted his favourite phrase: "I'll keep my **eyes** peeled for you." He now knows why a lot of the recipients look quite bewildered. Have you got a favourite phrase like that?

The NLP language of feeling

It **boils down** to money
We're skating on **thin ice**
He drives a **hard** bargain
It **slipped** my mind
What a **stuffed** shirt!
She's as **sharp** as a tack
It's too much **hassle**

And there is even a gustatory way of speaking used by all three of the other styles at times

The sweet **smell** of success
I can **taste** the opportunity
That's a **tasty** idea
You could **smell** their fear
I'll **chew** it over
Chances are they will **bite**
Success is **bittersweet**

A **warm and wonderful** day
He was **cool and calm,**
When did we last **touch** base?
Just do it!
We **pulled** some strings
Get a **load** of this
We came to **grips** with the problem
They were a **pain** in the neck
He was a **smooth** con man
They're **hand-in-glove**
You could **feel** energy
I'm not **following** you

Once **bitten,** twice shy
They **lapped** it up like cream
You catch more with **sugar than salt**
As **smooth** as ice cream
A small **morsel** of their business would be enough
It is our **bread and butter** and anything on top is **cream**
Catch a **whiff** of this
This smells **fishy** to me
He licked his **chops**

How many did you mark off in each?

A reminder: your highest score is your preferred style for speaking, writing and hearing. Your second highest score is your backup style. Many good communicators use all of the languages, all of the time.

Make persuasive communication happen for you

> *"Come quickly, I'm tasting stars."*
> Dom Perignon (1638–1715) at the moment of his discovery of champagne

With neurolinguistics, persuasive writing is yours for the doing. By incorporating see, hear, feel and some taste words into your copy, you can involve all your readers, just as easily as you can when speaking—more easily, perhaps, because you are able to rewrite words for a printed page.

> *"Honest criticism is hard to take, particularly from a relative, a friend, an acquaintance or a stranger."*
> Franklin P. Jones

As a useful beginning to using these three or four languages, go back into your files and pull out letters, reports, brochures, flyers and even invitations that have gone out in the past few months. Rewrite them, slipping in the three or four languages that you have learned from the past few pages. See if the copy now leaps off the page.

Deliberately seek out the companionship of someone whom you have never really liked, though you do not know why. Have coffee with them, talk with them and listen for their personal communication style. See if it is different from yours.

Remember that little rhyme:

> "I do not like thee, Dr Fell,
> The reason why I cannot tell,
> But this I know and know full well,
> I do not like thee, Dr Fell."

Now we know why: it's all in the way we and other people speak, hear and write.

When you see life as a process in which there are winners and losers, you can become a winner by understanding and meeting the unconscious needs of others. For instance:

1. When you go into a meeting, be very clear about what it is you want to achieve in this time. I mentally lock the door with my outcome as I enter a meeting and know that I cannot get out until I have achieved it or have come to a joint agreement on a variation.
2. Court the other person. Look, listen, feel and probe. Use the phrase "what is it?" and then repeat back their concerns about price, timing, delivery, colour, design—whatever. This will give you the sensitivity to know whether you are moving towards or away from your desired outcome. Acknowledge the reason to yourself.
3. Be flexible. Vary your approach according to the other person's needs. Nobody on earth sees, hears or feels exactly the way you do. We can never know the full facts behind another's wants, needs and desires. We can, however, probe and listen for sufficient clues to adapt.

   We did it naturally when we were children. We do it when we are in pursuit of an object of desire. We can do it in business.

Here is an example: A friend called me and said either she or her daughter would have to leave home, she couldn't stand it any more. She explained further—she had a loving, hugging, kissing relationship with her young son, but the daughter was constantly nagging at her, day and night, saying, "Mummy, Mummy, do you love me?" while pulling at her arm.

In response she would bend down and kiss her. Then the child would repeat her refrain. Obviously the feeling of a kiss was not her way of taking in love. I suggested she try saying, "Yes dear, I do", being an auditory response and if that didn't work, try giving her little gifts, being a visual response.

The next day she rang and said the auditory response had worked the miracle. The daughter came to the breakfast room, repeated her usual refrain, and her mother replied, "Yes dear, I do". The child then said, "Thank you, Mummy", and ran outside to play.

Similarly a highly visual client had trouble with his stepson, a feeling child who constantly demanded physical closeness by sitting almost on top of my client, holding onto him, following him around until he was ready to quit the new marriage.

In the end he decided to be the initiator of contact, putting his arm around the child, giving him a hug, inviting him on walks. When I asked him if it worked he said, "Yes, if I remember to do it".

Here's another one. At a business meeting with two associates, I was explaining the value of neurolinguistics and the husband said that he must be feeling as he loved their courtship days when they went hand in hand on their morning run.

His wife said she hated those runs, she was forever falling in the gutter and hurting herself. The husband was amazed—his treasured memory was her worst. So they started talking about her other feelings—anger and frustration at his homecoming; she got in a little earlier than he from work and was fully involved in getting dinner for the family when he arrived. Her complaint was that he rushed in, grabbed her and didn't even see that she was trying to juggle hot dishes around and had no need for sex at the same time.

The husband took all this in and then asked what would make her happy at that critical time. She replied that ideally he should come in, pass her a glass of white wine from the far side of the kitchen divider, blow her a kiss and set the table. Then help her with the dishes, the children's baths, getting them organised for school and into bed.

That done he could have her undivided attention. So the husband went out and bought her favourite white wine, some beautiful crystal glasses and chilled them both to perfection. Then he did all the other things she requested, and you have never seen two happier people. A visual person with a feeling husband and they both found delightful ways to compromise.

Success in any interaction

1. Put yourself into a top state. This means being physically and mentally alert, in tune with the other person's needs and your own.
2. Have a purpose, aim, direction or outcome for the interaction.
3. Establish rapport (more on which follows).
4. Have a plan as to how next to proceed.

Rapport is the ability to reduce to a minimum the unconscious difference between you and someone else. People do not have to like you to be in rapport with you.

What is important is that they feel comfortable with you on an unconscious level, which in the end probably means that they do like you.

Two aspects of rapport are pacing and leading

Pacing comes from matching certain aspects of another's behaviour, such as their verbal and body language, so that they begin to feel comfortable with you.

Once this happens the next step is **to lead** them in the direction you want them to move—this time by changing your voice tempo, your body language. Example: when someone is angry, you match their energy in body and voice, then lead them to a more gentle place, where you can discuss their problem more comfortably.

The secret of and reason behind seeking rapport is that we all feel most comfortable with those we perceive to be most like us.

Let us now try a further test with a new dimension. How do you respond to daily life: is it from seeing, hearing, feeling or—here's the new one—analysing?

For each of the following statements, place these numbers as follows:
4 beside the phrase that best describes you
3 beside the phrase that would be the next best description of you
2 beside the phrase that is next in your preference
1 beside the phrase that would least describe you.

1. Emotions, moods

I show my innermost moods and emotions to other people particularly by:

a. The clothes that I choose to wear _______ S
b. The feelings I share with those around me _______ F
c. The words I choose very carefully _______ An
d. The various tones of my voice _______ H

2. Music

I prefer to:

a. Tidy my tapes, discs and records in order of the artists and separate classical from jazz from modern, but not play them very often _______ An
b. Listen to music at home with others _______ H
c. Go to concerts whenever I want but only keep a small collection at home _______ S
d. Shut myself away and experience the music alone _______ F

3. You and the world around you

a. I am very sensitive to all the noises that surround me _______ H
b. It is easy for me to make sense of complicated facts and new information _______ An
c. I choose the fabrics that I wear by the way they feel on my body _______ F
d. I have a strong response to colours wherever I go, indoors and out _______ S

4. Making big decisions

I make big, important decisions, such as buying a house, based on:

a. My gut level feelings _______ F
b. Which choice sounds best to me _______ H
c. What looks best to me _______ S
d. A precise, extensive analysis of all the important issues _______ An

5. Communicating

During a serious discussion I am most likely to respond to:

a. The other person's manner and tone of voice ______ H
b. Whether or not I can see the other person's point of view ______ S
c. The continuing logic and sense of the other person's argument ______ An
d. Whether or not I feel in touch with the other person's feelings and emotions ______ F

6. Reading

Books appeal to me because:

a. I can read quietly by myself and enjoy the mood, the feelings, the emotions as they come up ______ F
b. I can have talking books in the car and on the player at home and listen at my leisure ______ H
c. I can literally see the book's story unfold before my eyes in full colour and be there ______ S
d. I can collect and keep relevant books on subjects of interest neatly sorted on the bookshelves and refer to them as needed ______ An

Write in your numbers from each of the six experiences:

	Seeing (S)	Feeling (F)	Hearing (H)	Analysing (An)
1. Emotions				
2. Music				
3. The world around you				
4 Decisions				
5. Communicating				
6. Reading				
Your totals				

The comparison of the score totals gives you your preferences for each of the four possible systems. You may be strong in one or two categories, or spread evenly among all four. As a quick and easy tool for identifying differences between individuals, you may find this quite useful in business management styles and in your relationships and family issues.

Here is one easy way of knowing whether or not the other person is responding positively towards what you are saying and doing: **pupil response**.

You will have noticed that pupil dilation or constriction is an extremely accurate indicator of a person's response to stimulation. You will have seen that when people are interested or aroused, their eyes open wider, their pupils dilate. When confronted with unpleasant or noxious stimuli, they narrow their eyes and the pupil constricts.

Even a mild arousal of interest will change the size of the pupil. Knowing what emotional states cause these fairly obvious changes can give you a special kind of insight into a person's internal state.

Another way to improve responses:

In the section on colour and design, we noted that what is seen on the right-hand side of the viewer is transferred to the left-hand side of the brain and vice versa. The left-hand side of the brain is the analytical, detail-facts-and-figures side of the brain. The right-hand side is the creative, sensitive, feeling side of the brain.

So it follows that it is important where you place an item for viewers to respond to it in the way you want. For instance, a contract should be placed to their right in order to transfer the logic, facts and detail to the left-hand side of the brain and thereby to get them ready to read and understand.

Creative work, such as a new advertising campaign or colour schemes for decorating an office or home, should be placed to the left, so that the information goes through to the right-hand, creative side of the brain, thus getting the viewer in a state of readiness for the colourful decisions to be made.

If you place information in the centre of the viewer's gaze there is a moment while they sort out what it is and decide how to respond, probably shifting the papers as they do so. Anything seen in the centre of the viewing scope diverts to both sides of the brain, thereby giving a neutral, possibly confused, response.

You may have heard people say, "What is this?" in a gruff, concerned tone of voice when you have plonked something down in front of them unexpectedly.

However if you dropped that unexpected piece of paper to their left or right, they would have at first glance sorted it through to the other side of the brain.

Chances are that they will then have to resort, depending on the content. It is far better to make the correct placement for them, so that any communication piece is received directly in the correct hemisphere of the brain, even before they have picked it up.

Similarly, if you wish to be taken seriously, move to that person's right so that you and your actions and words are processed on the left-hand analytical side.

If you are having a creative discussion, try to position yourself and your support material on the left of the person buying, so that your words and actions go through to their right-hand, creative side.

I have tested this with clients and taught it to hundreds of people. It works for me, and it could well do so for you. A right-handed person has a dominant left hemisphere; a left-handed person, a dominant right hemisphere.

You may have seen a predominance of left-handed people in creative environments, such as artists in studios, actors out to lunch together or advertising people who have set up a highly creative new agency.

They are often seen being creative—writing on the tablecloth, creating a drama about the food, showing off their colourful, trendy clothes.

Analytical, accounting people are usually right-handed, with the left-hand side of their brain working overtime. They are apt to be intellectual and analytical even at lunch, figuring out the grams of fat, the calories and the cost.

Here are some functions of the left hemisphere:

Sorting of detail; abstract, analytical, rational, linear, sequential, propositional, objective and successive thinking.

Some functions of the right brain are:

Intuitive, feeling responses; divergent, free, imaginative, creative, non-linear, subjective, simultaneous many-faceted thinking.

Billions of neurons make up the human nervous system. Even though sensory input varies from pressure to temperature to sound to colour, these are all ultimately transformed into electrochemical impulses as they are sent through to our central nervous system.

This means that our perception of reality is a neurological response to reality, and that gives us our individual perception of the world.

Because sensory organs vary greatly from one individual to another, each of us perceives the world differently. But since our perceptions form the basis for our models of the world, we can assume that every individual will have a different model.

On the other hand, our perceptions are similar because of similarities in neurological responses. Most people will agree that sugar is sweet, salt is not (though the intensity of sweet or salt will be different for each individual).

These similarities, combined with shared social and cultural experiences, make possible the creation of group realities. These shared realities form the basis of our social structures, of which language is a good example, even though the way people say words is often not the way we hear them. Thus, though we are like each other in many ways, none of us is exactly like any other person on earth.

Key points to remember

> *"Nothing is impossible for the man who doesn't have to do it himself."* A.H. Weiler

Understand others by understanding yourself. Use your knowledge of personality profiles and NLP to see, hear and feel what is going on around you.

Use these twelve steps and own your future in new-business development.

You can make it happen now. You can be the one who will pick up the phone every day, make a few phone calls and be consistent in pursuit, product, sound, colour, design, behaviour, communications. It is not difficult, but it is unusual.

More on NLP

(With thanks to my many NLP teachers)

The following is the training program that I use when consulting for companies on NLP. You need to have two or three people to use this material, though it works almost as well if you do it by yourself.

"The biggest block to rapport is thinking that because you see the world one way, everyone else does too. Excellent communicators rarely make that mistake. They know they have to change their language, their tonality, their gestures, until they discover an approach that is successful in achieving their outcome." Anthony Robbins, *Unlimited Power*.

Agenda:
Introduction

Establishing Rapport
1. Understanding representational systems
2. Eye accessing
3. What communicates your message?
4. Matching voice qualities
5. Non-verbal communication—mirroring

Influencing Others
6. Pacing and leading
7. Outcome/problem frame
8. Eliciting and utilising criteria
9. Anchoring techniques

Introduction
List the challenging situations you face, at home and at work, where your ability to influence others is important to your success.

1 ....

....

2 ....

....

3 ....

....

4 ....

....

5 ....

....

6 ....

....

7 ....

....

8 ....

....

9 ....

....

The learning process

1. When we are born we are unconsciously incompetent. We do not know how to do anything, and do not care! We simply make a fuss til someone comes along and fixes it.
2. As we get older we realise that we are struggling to do the simplest things, like feed ourselves, crawl, walk, run, speak. We are conscious of our incompetence and do care—hence the tears, tantrums, terrible twos.
3. Later we are consciously competent—we can read slowly, walk and talk carefully, feed ourselves somewhat, do up our buttons and tie our shoelaces—but we have to think about it as we do it. We can write, but only with a tightly gripped pencil and our tongue poking out.

4. Then as more time goes by, we become unconsciously competent—we can read, eat, walk, run, drive and do many other things without thinking. We have reached a new maturity. But every new skill we take on board has to start first with the semi-conscious or conscious awareness that we are incompetent at something—that we want to change to a better way of life.

We have to want to change or else we don't focus, learn, take on board the new ways. Hence we become very good at doing things that we have a passion or real liking for—and remain consciously incompetent at the things we dislike.

List some of the things you love to do and do well.

....

....

....

And some things you dislike doing and do badly.

....

....

....

Our goal is to learn more techniques for increasing sales, to become unconsciously competent at selling. Neurolinguistics is the key.

1. Understanding representational systems

Each of us experiences a constant stream of information being communicated to us by way of sensory communication channels (the five human senses of seeing, hearing, feeling, tasting and smelling).

We communicate with one another most frequently by using the three primary senses: visual or sight, auditory or sound, and kinesthetic or feelings or touch.

We call these sensory channels **representational systems** because they represent how a person is receiving external information and making sense of it internally.

People who communicate via **visual** representational systems **see** pictures and have images of their experiences.

People who communicate via **auditory** representational systems **hear** sounds and talk about their experiences.

People who communicate via their **kinesthetic** system experience internal or external sensations and have **feelings** about their experiences.

Equally important is the fact that not only do we see, hear and feel experiences being communicated to us from an external source, but the psychoanalyst Carl Jung heard in his counselling sessions that we also express such experiences by using specific language patterns which indicate the representational system we are using.

The words comprising such language patterns are called "predicates" and include verbs, adjectives and adverbs which are the parts of speech used for showing action, describing something, and telling how, when, and where.

People who describe their experiences visually usually use predicates such as "look", "see", "picture" or "perspective".

People who describe their experiences auditorially use predicates such a "hear", "say", "listen", "sound" or "talk".

People who describe their experiences kinesthetically use such predicates as "feel", "hold", "handle" or "grasp". Often, we unconsciously use the same sensory-based language in our speech that someone else does: we match each other's representational system and become easily absorbed in conversation.

However, there are times when we unconsciously "mismatch" someone else's representational system and then wonder why no rapport was established.

Herein lies the difference between those people who easily establish rapport and trust with others and those who do not.

In order to successfully establish high levels of rapport with another person, it is important to be able to identify and match the specific representational system or language patterns used to communicate.

The benefits you derive from this ability can be utilised in every area of your personal and professional life.

Describe in your own words a time when you felt in total rapport with another person. Where you were, what you were doing, why it was special.

....

....

....

The following examples of sensory-specific predicates reveal the various representational systems by which we communicate.

Visual
I **see** what you are saying.
That **looks** good.
This idea isn't **clear**.
I'm **hazy** about that.
I went **blank**.
Let's cast some **light** on the subject.
Get a new **perspective**.
Looking back, it **appears** differently.
It was an **enlightening (insightful, colourful)** example.

Auditory
I **hear** you.
It **rings** a bell.
It **sounds** good to me.
Everything suddenly **clicked**.
Listen to yourself.
The idea has been **rattling** around in my head.
Something **tells** me to be careful.
I can really **tune** into what you're saying.

Kinesthetic (feeling)
It **feels** right to me.
Get a **handle** on it.
Do you **grasp** the basic concept?
Get in **touch** with yourself.
I have a **solid** understanding of it.
I'm **up against** a wall.
Change your standpoint.
You're so **insensitive**.
I have a **feeling** you're right.
I am **boxed** into a corner.

Note that a person reading a holiday brochure can be representing their future experience in a variety of ways. They may see the sights of the holiday, imagine the sounds and tastes of skiing, swimming, sailing, drinking, eating and feel the sensations of all those activities, but at different levels of intensity.

In the following examples of representational systems, mark off those phrases that you would feel comfortable using in everyday language.

Visual
Lazy, **hazy** days of summer
This is an **obscure** and difficult text
It is all too **dim** and in the past
I agree with your **perspective**
We have let minor issues **cloud** our thinking
We gained **focus** through reviewing the document
The **picture** is clear now
Envision this new equipment
She is remarkable for her **vision**
We all have a different **viewpoint**
From my point of **view**
Come **look** at this
Gaze out the window
Illuminate us with your wisdom
Get a **glimpse** of this
Let me **illustrate** that point
We **perceive** them to be different
We will keep **watch** on their progress
Let them first **scan** the information
We need to **survey** the results first
The effect is **visible**
We can **see** the whole **picture** at a **glance**
The longer we **stare** at the mess, the less it will go away
Show me how you did it
That **looks pretty good** to me
Now I have got the **picture**
It is as **clear as mud**
The **after-glow** of a great presentation

Auditory
Hear me out
You are not **listening** to me
Talk me through the problem
I'm in **harmony** with your needs
It's coming through **loud** and clear
Shout it out
I **told** you that would happen

Post-purchase **dissonance** is allowed for in the contract
A resounding **yell**
Lend an **ear**
I bent his **ear**
You need to **amplify** that point
The **cadence and rhythm** of their song and dance act
Chatterbox
Whine and groan
All you ever do is **moan**
Hiss and foam of the sea
He **voiced** his opinion
We must **orchestrate** the presentation
Sounds like fun out there
The **silence** is killing me
I'm in **tune** with your ideas
Tone down the extravagance

Kinesthetic
Feel the **feeling**
So **warm** to **touch**
Can you **handle** the problem?
Grasp the nettle
A **tight** ship is a good ship
Smooth as silk
Rough and tumble of business
Cut and thrust of negotiaton
A **firm** hand at the helm
Apply **pressure** if they don't decide soon
Their **indecision** makes the situation tense
Concrete evidence
Hurt feelings
Handled **roughly**
He is **clumsy** with figures
She is **relaxed** about deadlines
It's a **swell** world we live in
Tremble at the sound of his voice
Shiver all over at that piece of music
Shake them up, get them going
Penetrate the puffery
Absorb the cost and fix the problem
Uncomfortable with dissent
Stir the masses

Agitated by lack of timeliness
Cutting remarks
Glow with pride
Flush with happiness
Itch to succeed
Creep up unannounced

Olfactory/Gustatory (smell/taste)
Sweet taste of success
The **flavour** of the month
Savour the moment
Relish the thought
Nice and **tangy**
A **palatable** offer
Leaves a **nasty aftertaste**
The **sweet smell** of success
Scent the breeze
A **whiff** of how it could be
Pungent with desire
The contract **stinks**
There's a **reek** of deceit
A **nose** for a good deal
Leave a **bad taste** in my mouth

Predicate Exercise I
Identify which system is being used in the following sentences.
Place a "V for Visual, "A" for Auditory and "K" for Kinesthetic beside each indented phrase.

I understand you ...
 What you are doing **feels** right to me
 I **see** what you mean
 I **hear** you **loud** and **clear**

I know ...
 I can **grasp** your meaning
 That really **clicks**
 I'm in **tune** with what you're doing
 That's **clear** to me
 That **fits** in
 I **catch** the idea
 That **rings** a bell

I have gained **insight**
I **see** your point
That **strikes** me as being correct
That's perfectly **clear**

That's confusing . . .
Show it to me in black and white
I can't make rhyme or **reason** of it
I'm trying to **take it in**
Sounds like **noise** to me

I don't understand . . .
It's **dim**
It **sounds** distorted
I can't get in **touch** with your needs

It seems obscure . . .
It doesn't **fit in**
It's all very **hazy** to me
That point is as **clear as mud**
It **sounds** garbled

Help me to understand . . .
It has **slipped away** from me
It's all **Greek** to me
I'm **straining** to get your meaning
It **sounds** like **gibberish**
I don't **see** your meaning

Predicate Exercise II
Mark each of the phrases as being an example of V, A, K, or O/G
I **feel** like I'm dealing with too many people
We **perceive** promotions happening less with less budget
We can do something to **ease** the pain
Should we **look** at other systems?
They **saw** the promotional opportunities
There is **light** at the end of the tunnel
I've been **hearing** a lot about the new Sunday paper
A lot of those new directives got **zapped**
We had a **voice** in the decisions
I'm **hearing** this person tell me that isn't so
Do you **see** it or don't you?

In my **observation**, the time wasn't right
The first three orders are **bread and butter**, after that it is all **cream**
The rest of the company didn't **focus** on the same area
It's just the way things have **fallen out**
The **sweet taste** of success
I can **smell the scent** of money

Predicate Exercise III

Step A:

1. Participant "A" generates a sentence using predicates from only one of the three main representational systems. (VAK)
2. Participant "B" mismatches A's predicates while maintaining an appropriate response.

Step B:

1. "A" repeats the same sentence.
2. "B" matches A's predicates.

Step C:

1. Repeat Steps A and B until all three sensory categories with matching predicates have been used.
2. Rotate positions. When each participant has generated sentences using all three systems, move on to Step D.

Step D:

1. "A" generates a sentence using a "sequence" of the various predicate systems.
2. "B" matches the sequence of predicates in response.
3. Repeat Step D using a different sequence of the various predicate systems. After three sentences have been accurately completed, change positions.

Record Your Experiences.
What did you experience when the practitioner mismatched the representational system that you were using?

....

....

....

....

Conversely, what happened when the practitioner matched the representational system you were using?

....

....

....

Group Discussion to Predicate Exercise III
So what does this mean? How can you use this insight to be a more effective communicator and presenter?

Example 1: The ability to adapt your language to the predicates of others is necessary to form good relationships at work and home. List some of these relationships:

....

....

....

Example 2: To establish rapport quickly, communicate most effectively, and influence a large group, the presenter must communicate in all three sensory channels. List some up-coming presentations and write in the dollar value to you when you win each account:

....

....

....

....

Add up total value when you win all that you listed:

....

....

Predicate exercise IV (Write out all your statements first if you wish, then read them aloud . . .)
First Person:
Describe your dream house or car or holiday, using mostly visual predicates. After four or five sentences . . .

Second Person:
Pick up the story, but use mostly auditory predicates.
After four or five sentences ...
Third Person:
Pick up the story using mostly kinesthetic predicates ...
First Person:
Begin a new story using only auditory predicates.
Second Person:
Pick up the story using only kinesthetic predicates ...
Third person:
Pick up the story using only visual predicates ... and so on, until each person has had experience using each type of predicate exclusively in several sentences of a story.

Outcome:
Discover which systems are easy for you to generate and which are more difficult. Note though, that you do have the ability to access all predicates, depending on your need to express a particular experience.

If you were at a concert, you might talk more about the sound of the piano rather than what the pianist was wearing (the visual aspect).

With Mick Jagger though, you might well talk in equal predicates about the sight of his frenetic energy, the noise of his music, and the excitement of being there—a totally involving experience.

2. Eye accessing

Accessing Cues (as you face the other person)

Diagram represents generalised human behaviour.

UP VISUAL (Constructed Imagery

EYES DEFOCUSED (Fixed position usually pupil dilation, visual imagery remembered or constructed)

UP VISUAL (Remembered imagery)

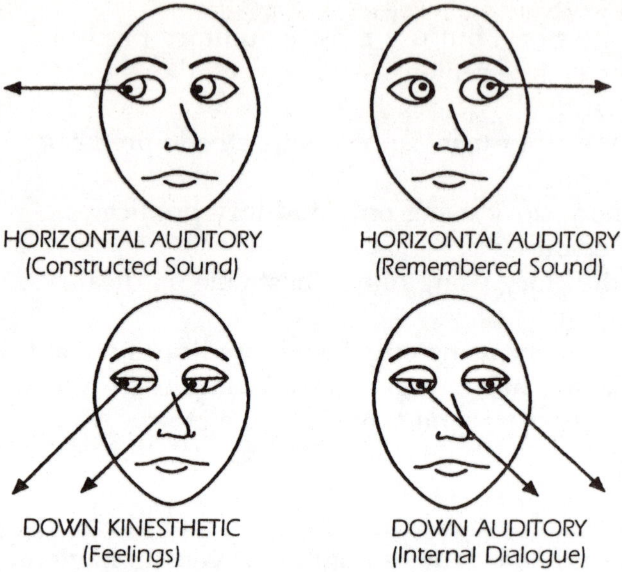

* *Note*: This schematic is reversed for left-handed people.

Visual representational system

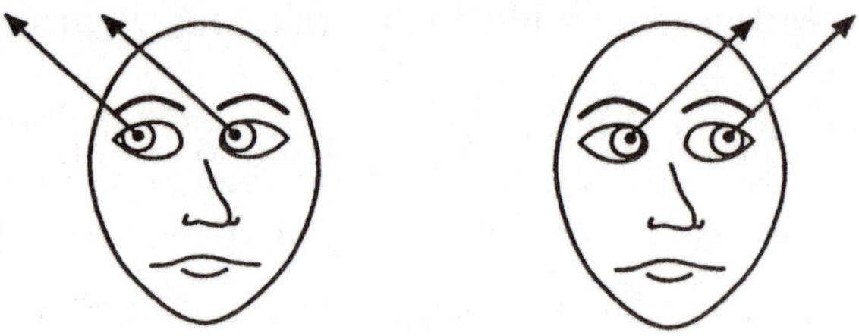

Voice:
Often high and fast.

Posture:
Neck extended, head tilted up, leans forward.

Gestures:
Up and out. Expansive to draw pictures in the air.

Breathing:
High in chest, shallow, rapid breathing.

Predicate Language:
Look, observe, view, scan, focus, glance, read, colours, watch, visualise, draw, light on, sight, peer, appear, daze, see, get the picture?

Auditory Representational System

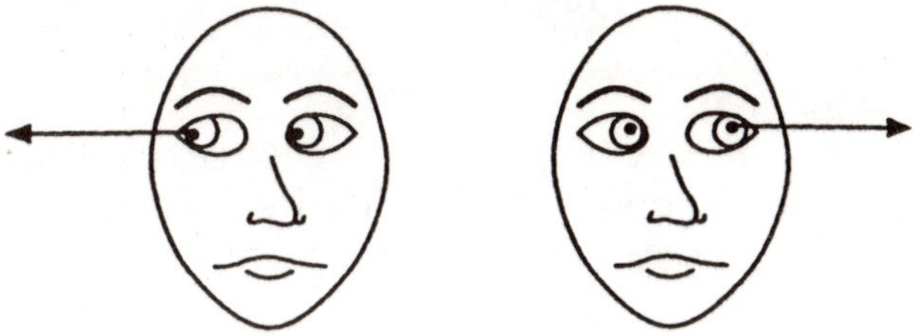

Voice:
Melodious, varied, soft, rhythmic.

Posture:
Head tilted to one side, favours one ear (telephone posture).

Gestures:
Hands near face, mouth, ears, jaw. Rhythmic to mark words.

Breathing:
Relatively deep, middle of chest, even in rate.

Predicate Language:
Say, speak, talk, declare, cry, reporting, utter, express, whisper, announce, hear, listen, tell, discuss, sounds, static, tone, music, in tune with me?

Kinesthetic Representational System (Feeling/ sensation)

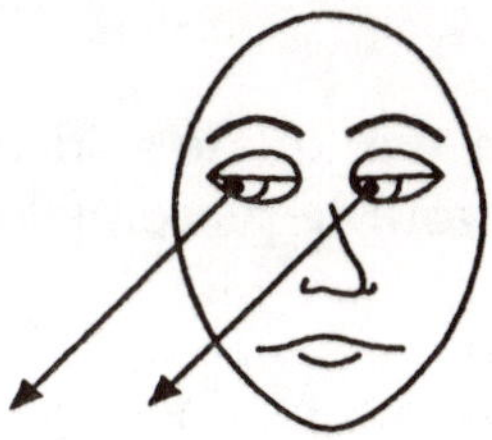

Voice:
Often deep. Words said slowly with pauses.

Posture:
Head and eyes often down. Body may slouch.

Gestures:
Hands folded on stomach or chest. Hand movements low.

Breathing:
Low from the belly and regular.

Predicate Language:
Feel, touch, handle, excited, aroused, reactive, expressive, sense, emotional, bear, anxious, dislike, desire, heavy, deep, walk, joined, active—can you grasp the idea?

Eye accessing exercise 1.
This exercise requires the participation of two people.

Step A.
"A" asks "B" the following questions and observes eye movements. A's objective here is to correlate the similarities and differences between the kind of information A is seeking and the non-verbal eye movements of B. If B gives responses which A does not understand, A should ask B what they were thinking.

Visual—Remembered
How many doors does your house have?
Where did you sit at home?
How many pairs of walking shoes do you own?

Visual—Constructed
How would you look with green-coloured hair.
Imagine the house you live in becoming three times larger.

Auditory—Remembered
Remember something a workmate said this morning.
Hear the sound of a favourite piece of music.

Auditory—Constructed
Listen to the sound of a child's whistle playing a familiar song.
What would you say if someone asked you how to eliminate childhood diseases.

Auditory—Digital—talking to yourself
Tell yourself what you have to do before you go to work tomorrow.
Tell yourself how you would benefit from learning a new language.

Kinesthetic—feeling
How did you feel this morning just when you got out of the shower?
How do you feel after you work out?

Olfactory/Gustatory—Smell/Taste
Remember the smell of Christmas dinner.
Remember the taste of your favourite ice cream.

Step B:
Switch positions and repeat the exercise.

Step C:
Make up your own questions to elicit visual, auditory or kinesthetic responses.

3. What communicates the message?

A mix of:
Voice tone
Words—especially with the understanding of NLP
Body language
Voice qualities

Voice Matching exercise
Step A:
"A" generates 2–3 sentences exaggerating the voice volume.

Step B:
"B" responds and mismatches the volume of the subject's voice.

Step C:
"A" continues speaking at same volume for 2–3 sentences.

Step D:
"B" responds back matching the volume level of A

Step E:
Repeat exercise, varying the rate of speech.
Switch roles.

Step F:
Complete questions 1 & 2.

1. How would you describe the experience when the practitioner mismatched the volume or tempo of your voice?

   ....

   ....

   ....

2. How would you describe the experience when the practitioner matched the volume or tempo your voice?

   ....

   ....

   ....

Group discussion on voice matching exercises

a. What generalisations can you make about voice matching?

   ....

   ....

   ....

b. How can you use this skill to make you a more effective communicator?

   ....

   ....

   ....

4. Non-verbal communication

Mirroring

Mirroring is a process used to "match" your own non-verbal behaviour and vocal tones (i.e. tone, tempo, pitch and volume, hand gestures, body posture) with that of another person.

By developing the skill necessary to mirror another's communication without it becoming obvious to him or her that you are doing so, you can effect an unconscious sense of trust on the part of that person and thereby establish higher levels of rapport.

Mirroring Exercise

This exercise requires the participation of a subject, practitioner and assistant.

Step A:
"A" recalls a past experience that was emotional (i.e. winning a race, the birth of a child, or a motor bike ride). Go back and re-live the experience as fully as you can.

Step B:
"B" matches the non-verbal aspects of "A". Mirror posture, muscle tones and place of breathing in the chest as closely as you can.

Assistant: Help "B" match the subject's non-verbals exactly. Maintain this posture for 30-60 seconds and imagine what would be happening to you right now in this body posture and expression. Guess what the subject is thinking. Find out if you are correct.

Step C:
Rotate positions until all have had the experience.

Step D:
Please record your experience here:

What happened when you matched the subject to this extent and tried to guess their thoughts?

....

....

....

....

....

....

Group discussion on mirroring exercise 1
What conclusions or interpretations can you make about this experience? So what does this mean?

....

....

....

How can this apply in your work to make you more successful with your clients?

....

....

....

....

....

....

Pacing and leading exercise
This exercise requires the participation of a subject and practitioner.

Step A:
"B" describes an issue with a client on which they are currently working. Include any objections the client has to what "B" is selling.

Step B:
"A" roleplays this individual.

Step C:
"B" establishes rapport by mirroring body posture, voice qualities and representational systems. Pay attention to eye accessing if the subject doesn't reveal specific predicates. Once rapport is established, influence the subject to your point of view.

Step D:
Rotate positions.

Comments about the exercise:

....

....

....

....

....

5. Problem outcome frame

This exercise works well with a partner, but can easily be done on your own.

Step A:
"A" identifies a problem in a few words, now wait for "B" to ask you the following questions and reply accordingly.

1. What is the problem?

   ....

   ....

   ....

   ....

2. What caused the problem?

   ....

   ....

   ....

   ....

3. How is this limiting you?

   ....

   ....

   ....

   ....

4. What are the long-term consequences of this situation if it continues?

   ....

   ....

   ....

   ....

5. Is this a recurring problem?

   ....

   ....

   ....

Step B:
"B" now asks "A" the following set of questions and writes in the response.

1. What are three possible solutions?

   a ....

   b ....

   c ....

2. Which of these do you prefer?

   ....

   ....

   ....

3. What will that do for you?

   ....

   ....

4. How can you make it happen for you?

   ....

   ....

   ....

5. How can you use this obstacle to make you more successful?

   ....

   ....

   ....

6. How will this experience benefit you in the future?

   ....

   ....

   ....

Group Discussion:
In what situations would you want to use questions from the "problem cause" frame?

....

....

In what situations would you want to use questions from the problem solution/outcome frame?

....

....

....

6. Listening for criteria and using criteria to influence

Criteria exercise
This exercise requires the participation of a practitioner, subject and observer.

Step A:
"A" (Practitioner) asks "B" (Subject) the following questions. Listen for their criteria (answers) and take notes.
Observer (C) does likewise.
Q. Why did you choose to buy your current automobile?

....

....

Q. Why did you choose your last holiday?

....

....

Q. If you were hiring someone to do your job, what personal qualities would you look for? Of those qualities, which is most important?

....

....

....

If you had a free afternoon, with all the money you wanted, how would you spend the time? . . .Why did you choose that activity? What would that do for you?

....

....

....

Step B:
Practitioner and Observer plan a presentation to sell the Subject a gizmo for $5000.00.

Step C:
Practitioner sells the gizmo to the Subject using the criteria elicited from the conversation.

Exchange places until all have been sold to.

Group Discussion on Exercise I—Gizmo: how did you feel about selling and buying?

....

....

....

....

....

....

7. Anchoring technique

Definition: Anchoring is the process of attaching a stimulus (V, A or K) to a response.

Anchoring occurs when a specific stimulus such as a sound, a touch, a smell, a taste or a visual gesture becomes associated with an experience.

The Chinese, for instance, whisper in their child's ear when the child is being naughty. Soon the sight of an adult bending down to whisper stops them in their tracks.

Johnny Carson used to anchor his audience with a golf swing. He never had to say, "Let's go".

The best time to create an anchor is when rapport is at its highest peak. You can use key words, specially emphasised phrases, smile, point a finger, tap the table, raise your eyebrows or snap your fingers. Then you can bring back that high rapport instantly by using the same verbal or non-verbal cue when the time is right.

To make your anchoring even more effective, try to match your anchor to your client's predominant thinking mode. If your client is visual, use visual anchors like smiling, pointing a finger in the air or nodding your head.

For auditories, you can snap your fingers, clap your hands, tap objects, make your voice strong and excited.

For kinesthetics, who respond very much to touch, use a pencil or your finger, but keep it to near the elbow. Lower down the arm can be too intimate.

For yourself you can anchor a time when you felt terrific by recalling that time, and pressing your fingernail into your first knuckle. Then any time you want to recall that time, you simply rub that knuckle. Great for going into presentations, before you serve at tennis, facing up to a difficult client, or just enjoying life every day.

List examples of anchors that you would feel comfortable with:

....

....

....

....

....

....

....

Group Discussion:
In what context could you use anchoring to give you more influence?

....

....

....

....

....

....

....

....

Now in your own words, write how you think this NLP training will help you, using your own preferred languages(s).

....

....

....

....

....

....

....

See, hear and feel success.

Key points to remember

Understand others by understanding yourself. Use your knowledge of personality profiles and neurolinguistics to see, hear and feel what is going on around you.

Use the twelve steps explained in this book, and own your future in new-business development. You can make it happen now and forever. You can be the one who will pick up the phone every day, make a few phone calls and be consistent in pursuit, product, sound, colour, design, behaviour, communications. It is not difficult, but it is unusual.

And next for some case studies to explain some of the activities and results in a way that will bring a sense of reality to the twelve steps. These steps have been used, tested and proven over many years. Good luck, good hunting. See, hear and feel success.

> *"The first and great commandment is: don't let them scare you."* Elmer Davis

Put It All Together

Case studies

> *"Almost everyone who has become a great success in our society has been willing to take risks, and when they failed, were willing to try again, and again, and again."*
>
> W. Mitchell

While working with the Inter-Continental Hotel Group in Melbourne in the 1970s, I had been very successful in building the sales of room nights into the Inter-Continental hotels worldwide because of reward and recognition and good systems, plus of course a good product.

This is how I did it: I kept track of the room night sales from each travel agent in Melbourne. At the end of each month I went to the top-selling four and thanked each person for their support, offering chocolates. I started with the manager of the office, then on to the international travel staff and across to the receptionist. I also gave chocolates to the staff on local room night sales as they helped fill the Melbourne hotel.

I knew that in due course the receptionist and the local selling staff would move up to international travel consulting—and guess which hotel group they would then favour?

When there was a change in hotel information I updated their Inter-Continental information book for the travel consultants. I took the top-selling groups to lunch at the Melbourne hotel. I imported huge bunches of orchids from Singapore at New Year and just when everyone was feeling bored and lousy on the second of January, I would walk in with armloads of beautiful flowers, inviting the travel staff to take not one, but a handful.

Known as the "orchid and chocolate lady", I saw the outstanding effect these activities had, but only so long as the momentum was maintained.

Over a year of my life with Saatchi & Saatchi Hong Kong was devoted to promoting the Pampers disposable diaper. The client, Procter & Gamble, wanted to be market leader and at that time had a thirteen per cent market share. In Hong Kong there were around one hundred and twenty thousand mothers with babies of a diapering age. We set ourselves the target of finding about one hundred thousand families and putting all their details into the computer, thus creating a database of mothers and babies.

An all-out campaign was mounted. We used radio, TV and press to advise mothers that if they bought the Pampers product, trimmed the picture of baby's face off the pack (as proof of purchase) and sent that in with the coupon and their full name and address, we would send them a very attractive refund.

Interestingly, radio advertising with a male voice announcing the offer drew almost double the response of two female voices chatting about the offer.

It seems that the reason why men's voices are used more successfully in advertising is that as children we were constantly nagged at by our mothers. If we were really naughty, it was, "Wait until your father comes home". When he did there was a loud bellow and a lot of roaring.

Hence we listen to the male voice of authority and ignore the female nagging voice. The results of this advertising campaign seemed to prove the point that mothers, fathers and children are the same all over the world.

As the names and family details came into the computerised database we used a promotional technique in which these mothers were invited to fill in the form we mailed to them, with the names of other mothers, for a cash reward. In sales promotion this is known as "Friend Get a Friend" or in this case, "Mother Get a Mother".

For our next activity we invited mothers to "write their own cheque", in which they could claim refunds of up to Hkg$100 for multiple purchases of the disposable diaper. This was highly successful and generated more names for the database.

Back to the media. We tested *T.V. Week* and *Motherhood and Childcare* for a major advertising campaign. *T.V. Week* was about one-third the cost of *Motherhood and Childcare* and gave us about double the response. The cost/benefit analysis gave us the guideline for future advertising decisions.

The next stage was to go into hospitals and meet with new mothers. We decided to have a gift box for mothers containing long-term price discounts on the Pampers diaper and also on a face and body cream for the mother. (This product, Oil of Ulan/ Olay, was manufactured by another Procter & Gamble company.)

The single-minded proposition for the gift box was: "To see me is to want me."

Our professional hospital visitors would carry the gift box as they walked around the maternity wards. Hong Kong mothers love blonde, blue-eyed babies and it was this motif that we used on the gift pack. Truly, to see it was to want it. The mothers were delighted with the pack, the offers and the information inside. Again, up went the numbers in the database.

Next we arranged to be in the centres where the babies' births were registered. Free samples with discount coupons were distributed and again further increases in the database names. Additionally the company supported pre-natal and post-natal classes and more names were collected. We were approaching the target of one hundred thousand names by now.

Here's how I wrote up the process as a case study outline:

Product: Pampers disposable diaper.

Need: To make this brand the leading disposable diaper in Hong Kong.

Activities: 1. Obtain the names of one hundred thousand mothers of infants up to three years through continuous in-store, hospital, birth registry and pre- and post-natal clinic promotions, plus continuous advertising in relevant, tested magazines and on radio and TV. Special offers required the mothers to apply with full name and home address details for the item (for both Pampers and the Oil of Ulan/Olay face and body lotion).

2. Form a "Baby Club" and contact those mothers by mail on a three-monthly cycle, leading them to an educated understanding of the product and the need to move up to the next size each three months, as the baby grew.

Results: Pampers' market share grew from thirteen per cent to thirty-two per cent in the first year, an increase of US$19 million in sales.

The demand for the product was such that market share would have been fifty-two per cent (a US$42 million increase) but the factory was unable to supply. I noted that another reason for the shortage of product in Hong Kong was that it was being sold on the black market in Taiwan—a country in which we were not promoting it at all. While not what we had in mind, it was certainly a compliment to our work!

On to London, where I joined MSL, a Saatchi-owned executive recruitment company. MSL had been market leader in their twenty-five years in business, but had grown a little complacent and had lost market share to more aggressive, innovative companies. Using the Saatchi three-month (or less) cycle, we went to work changing their image and market position. Here is the brief case study:

Product: Executive search, advertised selection and recruitment advertising.

Need: To revamp image from old, established to pro-active, innovative, forward-thinking.

Activities: 1. Analysed existing client base (see section in this book on the Commonality Survey) and found that all were small to middle-sized companies. Further research indicated a fear of approaching the big companies as staff felt insecure talking to the gods of industry. The company agreed that this could be overcome with training.

A target list of four hundred major companies and six hundred relevant executives was created from in-house focused research on what the current best clients had in common.

2. I then wrote a survey on "Recruitment Issues of the 1990s" in which there were twenty-nine significant items, including job-sharing, benefits for part-timers, maternity/paternity leave, childcare, superannuation rights, training needs, effective performance reviews. Launched results at a lunch at the

Savoy. Three hundred and fifty major companies had filled in the surveys out of the five hundred distributed.

3. From these survey results we formed breakfast working parties in the MSL boardroom where those interested could share experiences and solutions to recruitment concerns and policies. Approximately one hundred and twenty human resources people attended per month.

4. Open Days every three months brought these and many other senior executives into the MSL offices to review processes such as psychological appraisals, team role models, the recruitment advertising creative processes—and, of course, to meet the staff.

5. Held half-day workshops for senior corporate executives, with major speakers such as Professor Charles Handy and Sir John Harvey-Jones. Attended to capacity. Participation offered at cost to ensure high level of attendance.

Results: Ten significant new accounts were won. One senior executive commented that he had never heard of our company before—and now he was having nightmares about us!

On to New York on assignment with a company (IMCOR) that was in contract management. With this service, executives are leased out temporarily to corporations in need of a senior person quickly, to take up an opportunity or fix a problem.

Product: A contract management/interim executive service supplying senior executives on temporary assignments across America.

Need: To install a regular, relentless contact system to add to existing networking by the four partners.

Activities: 1. Identified commonalities of existing client base. From this defined further prospects and established a database of eight thousand companies across America. In this instance the most likely users of the service were small to medium-sized companies, as large corporations already had an oversupply of senior executives.

2. Corporate literature was redesigned and rewritten. Colours used were royal blue (to look solid, stable, secure and here-forever in spite of only having been in business for three years), with a large block of white copy (in contrast) down the right-hand side of the front cover, explaining the service and its uses. (You will remember that when the copy is placed on the right-hand side it goes directly through to the left-hand, analytical side of the brain. The company is therefore perceived as being solid, stable, secure and here-forever.)

A regular, relentless contact pattern was established within the three-month cycle, in which the large new royal blue brochure (versus the old small cream one) was mailed with a covering letter. Then phone follow-up for appointments for the partners.

The special offer was a full credit of interim fees against the permanent fees, if the contract/interim manager became a full-time employee. This happened so often that it was promoted as "executive tryout". The deduction of the contract fees from the permanent placement cost was therefore a very significant offer. It allowed all parties to recognise that a permanent placement was possible, even to working out the costs beforehand.

3. Identified relevant conferences for niche markets, such as the financial sector. Achieved high visibility at these conferences through a planned program of sponsorship and contact before, during and after the meeting dates, advising of the contract management/interim services. Committed to three conferences, two months apart, to implant the product message.

Results: Combined with highly successful PR activities, the regular, relentless marketing program raised the company's profile to that of market leader in America. Acceptance of appointments with the partners reached a ratio as high as seven out of ten by the third round of mailing and phone contact, as the product was new and there was a great need for temporary senior executives. IMCOR was then able to consider franchising their service across America and beyond.

Now back to Australia, where my client, Thomas Cook, had a traditional base of older English-background clients. Thomas Cook was aware that their sales were now predominantly in air travel, although they had previously been very strong in cruising and coach tours.

Product: High-profile travel agent, with travellers' cheque division. Owned by the Midland Bank UK at that time.

Needs: 1. Thomas Cook had been pre-eminent in cruising sales but had slipped back over the years and wished to regain its position.

2. Thomas Cook had a large base of older clients and wanted to expand into the youth area. A broader base would protect it against the ageing of its traditional clients and increase its range of product sales.

Activities: 1. We researched favourite travel activities of the youth market and cruising showed up strongly. As a result Thomas Cook mounted a campaign with Sitmar, centred around their Bankstown travel shop. This area has a considerable number of young people who were easily accessible in the town square at lunch time and through their office jobs.

2. Travel staff dressed in nautical clothes distributed invitations to the staff of Bankstown businesses to attend a free Sitmar disco at a local venue. The tickets were available only through Thomas Cook's Bankstown travel office. Names, addresses and phone numbers of the applicants were captured at that time. The invitations were particularly attractive, with a colourful cocktail drink parasol neatly attached to the outside, as well as excellent special offers if bookings on Sitmar were made within six months.

3. The disco was run by Thomas Cook and Sitmar staff and a top disc jockey. The evening reflected the fun of the Sitmar experience and was attended by around five hundred young employed people in Bankstown.

Result: The Bankstown office became the top-selling Thomas Cook office for Sitmar and P & O cruises plus Royal Viking. Parents of the youth who had attended the disco now booked their P & O and Royal Viking cruises through the Bankstown office. Children and friends leaped aboard for more of the Sitmar experience. The local newspaper covered the event well, from our initial contact with a press release.

Follow-up contact included telephone research as to what had most pleased the young people attending. Results showed that they had loved the fine quality of the invitation, were delighted with the presence of the bouncers whom we hired for the occasion and felt very safe, secure and welcomed, so they would cruise with Sitmar at any time. No-one had any complaints. It is interesting that the quality of the bouncers came up so often. In doing youth promotions, it seems very important to give them good, safe fun in a large crowd.

We did follow-up mailings within three months to those who had attended, to remind them of the special offers. Another follow-up letter and brochure went out again in another three months to those who had not yet booked, and they were contacted regularly thereafter with other special offers.

The problem with the youth market is that addresses change more often than with older people and far more mail was returned. However, the young grow older and become more stable, book higher-price ticket items and become the senior citizens of the future. Moral of the story: bring them in young.

Now an exciting experience further down-under in the new South Africa. In Johannesburg an ABSA bank branch was losing 100 clients a week. My job was to be their education officer. Always ready for the new, I spent one of the most interesting periods of my life working with the staff there to turn the branch around. Here's the good news!

Needs: Stop the rush away from the branch. With one hundred or so clients a week moving on, through immigration **and** dissatisfaction, we could change only the latter reason. Training had to be in the evening, because the day's work had to be done, daily!

Activities: First the staff read this book, then night after night we worked through the twelve steps, first doing the SWOT analysis so that we could identify the key issues for the branch. Like virtually all companies I have worked with around the world, one of the major problems is that the staff were not involved in the business or marketing plans, therefore felt they had no control over the success or failure of the branch. At the end of the study period came the big question: "Of all the things we have reviewed together, what would you like to spend more time on?" I asked.

The answer surprised me. "Business plans and marketing plans." When I queried their choice, they replied that they spent most of their working life on family banking needs and did not really understand how businesses worked. They therefore hesitated to contact the business community in their area.

We then did a business plan together to grow the branch, and marketing plans to promote specific products.

Next:

The staff decided to target personal loans—a product of which they previously sold around two a month. They set themselves targets—a minimum of twenty personal loans for the month, maximum forty loans.

The staff contacted the community through advertising in local papers, household letterbox drops, posters and information in the branch and through talking directly to staff in the regional office and other banks, plus friends, family, relatives and of course, clients.

The result: Sixty-five personal loans were signed up in one month. "We're geniuses!" they said to me with glee. And indeed they were.

More results: The staff went on to target nursery school parents to take out educational funds for their children, then into old age homes to help clients too old to travel to better invest their funds.

They hand-wrote cards to people whose fixed deposits had passed their due dates and hence were earning no interest. Having previously sent official letters and phoned, they were amazed at the near 100% response to the handwritten cards. It seemed the only clients who did not respond were those whose addresses had changed.

Final result: A branch that had been losing around one hundred clients a week through immigration and dissatisfaction moved to **putting on over** one hundred clients per week. Encouraged by training and incentives, they went on to earn a good bonus—just in time for Christmas.

They had taken responsibility for defining their promotional activities, for writing the copy, designing the layout and even walked their talk by delivering the household letterbox drops.

For myself, I learned that empowering people to create their own destiny is all about having the business skills to define the direction, make the decisions, and get on with making it happen. People do truly want to work well and be effective—they only need the skills to make it happen.

Magic moments

Just occasionally something unexpectedly excellent happens and because of it, you remember with pleasure the person and the company they represent forever. For instance, in London I had a very pleasant meal at the Dorchester Hotel and the bill was more than reasonable. I commented to the waiter that I thought I had been undercharged and he replied: "If you have, Madam, it has been our pleasure." Mine too.

When I returned to Australia from New York, I wanted to test drive the (then) new Mazda Astina hatchback. Living on Sydney's upper north shore at the time, I somehow managed to ring the distant, outer west Blacktown showroom. Yet they offered to bring the car over for a test drive. All the way from Blacktown?

I expressed my surprise later to the salesperson, Daniel Eagen, and he said that since Blacktown was so far from everywhere, they had decided that the only way to sell to prospects was in their own homes. Yes, I did buy their Mazda. Their service and care were excellent all the way.

The point of these two stories is, of course, that it is not hard to stand out in the crowd. If you want to be a market leader in your field, it only takes common sense and some gentle good manners.

The hotel story is exceptional in that the waiter took the initiative not to worry about a small amount of money and did it so politely. The Mazda story is one of rare common sense that turned a disadvantage into a selling point.

Compare that experience with this: the same day that I rang Mazda at Blacktown, I test drove a Nissan nearby. The sales manager told me that I had to make up my mind by the weekend as the prices went up on Saturday! This is the oldest sales technique in the book, so guaranteed that I would not buy.

Recommended reading

You have just finished my overview of the marketing and selling techniques required to make your company successful. I hope it will be the beginning of an interesting and exciting voyage into a world of integrated marketing and relationship-building.

To help you on your way with more in-depth knowledge on all the necessary subjects, I put together the following list of top-selling books in each of the subjects covered in this book, plus some extras that may be well worth your time. Good luck and good reading! Thank you for joining me on this voyage.

Advertising Skills:

Albert C. Book & C. Dennis Schuck. *The Fundamentals of Copy & Layout*, NTC, 1988

Claude C. Hopkins. *My Life in Advertising*, NTC Books, 1987

Herschell Gordon Lewis. *The Art of Writing Copy*, Prentice Hall, 1989

David Ogilvy. *Ogilvy on Advertising*, Pan Books, 1983

Business Plans:

William S. Birnbaum. *If Your Strategy is so Terrific, How Come it Doesn't Work*, Amacom, 1990

Ron Johnson. *The 24 hour Business Plan*, Hutchinson, 1990

Kenichi Ohmae. *The Mind of the Strategist*, McGraw-Hill, 1982

Business Writing:

Laura Brill. *Business Writing Quick and Easy*, Amacom, 1989

Thelma Mansell. *How to Write Business Letters and Reports*, Pitman, 1990

Gladys Snodgrass & Elizabeth Murphy. *Letter Writing Simplified*, Pitman, 1986

Colour—Its Effect on You and in Business:

Dr Max Luscher, translated by Ian Scott. *The Luscher Color Test*, Washington Square Press/Pocket Books, 1987

Kenneth H. Mills and Judith E. Paul. *Applied Visual Merchandising*, Prentice Hall, 1988

Contact Management:
Lee Boyan. *Successful Cold Calling*, Amacom, 1989

Customer Service:
William H. Davidow & Bro. Uttal. *Total Customer Service*, Harper Perennial, 1990
Carl Sewell. *Customers for Life*, Pocket Books, 1990
Richard C. Whitely. *The Customer Driven Company. Moving from Talk to Action*, Century Business, 1991
V. Zeithami. *Delivering Quality Service*, Free Press, 1989
Ron Zemke and Chip R. Bell. *Managing Knock Your Socks Off Service*, Amacom, 1992

Direct Marketing:
Drayton Bird. *Commonsense Direct Marketing*, Kogan Page, 1988
Charles Mallory. *Direct Mail Magic*, Crisp Publications, 1991
Bob Stone. *Successful Direct Marketing*, NTC, 1989

Management Skills:
Stephen R. Covey. *The 7 Habits of Highly Effective People*, The Business Library, 1992
Peter Senge. *The Fifth Discipline. The Art and Practice of the Learning Organisation*, Random House, 1991
Michael J.S. Spendolini. *The Benchmarking Book*, Amacom, 1992

Marketing Plans:
Laura M. Dirks & Sally H. Daniel. *Marketing Without Mystery—a Practical Guide to Writing a Marketing Plan*, Amacom, 1991

Market Research:
Michael Baker. *Research for Marketing*, MacMillan, 1991
Paul Hague & Peter Jackson. *Marketing Research in Practice*, Kogan Page, 1992

Neurolinguistics:
Johnson, Kerry. *Selling with NLP. The revolutionary new sales techniques that will double your volume*, Positive Paperbacks, Nicholas Brealey Publishing, London, 1994
Byron Lewis and Frank Pucelik. *Magic of NLP Demystified*, Metamorphous Press, 1990

Psychological Profiling:
Isabel Briggs Myers. *Gifts Differing,* Consulting Psychologists Press, 1980

Public Relations:
Roger Hayward. *All About Public Relations,* McGraw-Hill, 1991
Tymson & Sherman. *The Australian and New Zealand Public Relations Manual,* Millennium Books, 1996

Sales Promotion:
Julian Cummins. *Sales Promotion,* Kogan Page, 1989

Self-Promotion:
Victoria Seitz. *Your Executive Image—the Art of Self Packaging,* Bob Adams Inc, 1991

Selling Skills:
Mack Hanan. *Consultative Selling,* Amacom, 1990
Michael Hewitt-Gleeson. *NewSell,* Wrightbooks, 1990
Robert B. Miller et al. *Strategic Selling,* Warner Books, 1985
Larry Wilson with Hersch Wilson. *Changing the Game: The New Way to Sell,* Fireside, 1988

Small Business Management:
T.F. Gaffney. *First Steps in Small Business,* Butterworths, 1990

Telephone and telemarketing:
Lloyd C. Finch. *Telephone Courtesy & Customer Service,* Crisp Publications, 1990
Julie Freestone & Janet Brusse. *Telemarketing Basics,* Crisp Publications, 1989

Time Management:
Roger Black. *Getting Things Done,* Michael Joseph, 1987
Merrill E. Douglas, Donna N. Douglas. *Manage Your Time, Your Work, Yourself,* Amacom, 1985
William Oncken Jr. *Managing Management Time,* Prentice Hall, 1984
D. Scott. *Time Management and the Telephone,* Crisp Publications, 1987